HURT YOURSELF

HARRY HURT III

In Executive Pursuit of Action,

Danger, and a Decent-Looking

Pair of Swim Trunks

HURT
YOURSELF

ST. MARTIN'S PRESS ≈ NEW YORK

www.stmartins.com

The essays in this book, with minor changes, first appeared as a series of columns in *The New York Times* between 2005 and 2007.

Library of Congress Cataloging-in-Publication Data

Hurt, Harry.
    Hurt yourself : in executive pursuit of action, danger, and a decent-looking pair of swim trunks / Harry Hurt III.—1st ed.
        p.   cm.
    "The essays in this book, with minor changes, first appeared as a series of columns in the New York Times between 2005 and 2007"—T.p. verso.
    ISBN-13: 978-0-312-38456-2
    ISBN-10: 0-312-38456-4
    1. Hurt, Harry. 2. Journalists—United States—Biography.
I. Title.
    PN4874.H838A3 2008
    070.92—dc22
    [B]

                                                          2008024265

First Edition: October 2008

10   9   8   7   6   5   4   3   2   1

FOR HARRISON

CONTENTS

PREFACE

Hurt Yourself is the world's first "self-hurt" book. As such, it is the dialectical opposite and blood-sworn enemy of all self-help books. It comprises twenty-four "Executive Pursuits" columns published in *The New York Times* between the summer of 2005 and the summer of 2007. But it is not merely a collection of separate pieces. It is the now-unified nonfiction narrative of an ongoing personal quest I conceived with madness aforethought.

Unbeknownst to my *Times* editors, I always had a secret plan. Without revealing too much, let's just say that the choices of subjects for my newspaper columns and the order in which they appeared were not merely coincidental. They were all part of a self-deprecating grand design that is continuing to unravel before my mind's eye.

Hurt Yourself is based on the premise that life is a high-pain, low-gain proposition that can be just or unjust but always boils down to just us. It is about participating in life to the fullest extent possible and surviving long enough to commiserate about it over a snifter of Cognac and a premium cigar. It is about exposing yourself to action, danger, humiliation, complete embarrassment, and, often worse, agonizingly incomplete embarrassment.

I've long since become accustomed to embarrassment: I've been stuck with the last name Hurt since birth. People have been making fun of it (and me) my entire life. That life began on November 13, 1951, in Houston, Texas, and has since taken me on a fool's cruise through forty-nine states and three continents. During my misinformed formative years, I was a house painter, a forklift driver, a hippie, a songwriter, a realtor, and a golf pro—in short, virtually everything but the lawyer or investment banker my dearly departed parents wanted me to be.

Perhaps even more disappointingly to them, I've also been a writer and a journalist, which explains my current predicament. I've squandered an otherwise promising prep school and Ivy League education to cover oil spills in Alaska, earthquakes in San Francisco, OPEC meetings in Ecuador, and financial shenanigans in New York, Chicago, London, Rotterdam, and Henderson, Texas. I've interviewed priests, rabbis, both president Bushes, and Fidel Castro. But I draw my true inspiration from interviews with murderers, prostitutes, and the late comedian George Burns, a fellow cigar smoker.

As of this writing, I reside in what I call Château Bow-Wow, a.k.a. the Doghouse. Château Bow-Wow is both a state of mind and an actual place located in the historic district of Sag Harbor, New York. It is a 150-year-old former butcher shop, ten paces long and maybe five paces wide, with clapboard siding and a peaked roof covered with asphalt shingles. It hunkers like a sheep-killing hound directly across the driveway from the main house.

I seem to occupy Château Bow-Wow up to forty-eight hours a day, eight days a week. If the reasons for that aren't already obvious, they soon will be. Château Bow-Wow is where I retreat to celebrate the triumphant moments of joy I occasionally manage to eke out of life, and where I lick the physical and emotional wounds I so very often inflict upon myself in the process. It is also where I conceived and wrote my columns for *The New York Times*.

The genesis of "Executive Pursuits" began in the winter of 2005 with the notion of facing fears with fun. *The Wall Street Journal* had just announced plans to publish a new weekend edition with lots of lifestyle content the following September. The *Times* determined to build up its Saturday edition, particularly the business section. James Impoco, a *Times* editor I'd known for several years, asked me to write an executive lifestyle column under the direction of his colleague Mickey Meece.

Rather than making "Executive Pursuits" a conventional newspaper column, we decided to model it partly on the television program *Saturday Night Live*. Back in 1977, *SNL* had made its debut in what was then considered a dead time slot at 11:30 P.M. Likewise, we were launching a column in what had previously been considered a dead zone in the *Times*. We figured it would have to be informative, but also edgy and irreverent. Our motto was "Live from New York! It's Saturday Business!"

Next thing I knew, I became a fire-eating, ballet-dancing, polo-playing yogi quarterback with $1,200 Italian shoes, double-breasted custom suits, and an insatiable passion for flying upside down. Although I recounted my pursuits in the first person, I quickly realized they were not about me. They were about what it's like to do _____. I was merely the reader's alter ego, filling in the blanks in our shared experiences.

Along the way, I also realized that being Hurt is a blessing in disguise. After all, what bond is more common among human beings than being hurt? Every man, woman, and child who ever lived has been Hurt at one time or another; those who are still alive will probably be Hurt soon again. That means there is hope in being Hurt—and power.

Hurt Yourself presents itself in six acts that begin with a film noir detective mission and culminate in a nearly disastrous scrape with deliverance. Act One tells a tale of custom suits, bling, and unexpected bliss in Chinatown. Act Two navigates through a series of close shaves that inevitably lead back to Château Bow-Wow, a.k.a. the Doghouse. Act Three poses—and once and for all answers—the philosophical question, "Is Anybody Necessary?"

Act Four soars on the wings of a World War II vintage fighter plane only to crash into the quicksand of parenting and the dilemma of buying a decent-looking pair of swim trunks. Act Five pays tribute to the participatory sports journalism legacy of the late George Plimpton and the leg warmers of the late ballet master George Balanchine. Act Six jump-cuts from Hollywood to hot dog vending to eating fire and capsizing in river rapids.

I mean all this to be a prelude of more things to come. I am intent on making up for all the time I've lost or simply don't remember. I aim to transform Hurt into shorthand for a universal human predicament. This book is the first volume in a larger continuing saga whose form and content are still being shaped by forces far beyond the reach of Mission Control back in my native Houston. Suffice it to say for the time being, that once you've Hurt yourself as I have, you just might find, as I have, that you're bound to Hurt yourself again and again.

Act One

CHINATOWN QUARTET

I'm Here to See a Man About a Suit

I went looking for a custom suit like some wiseacre detective named Jake in a film noir, only to wind up in Chinatown on the hottest damn day of the summer so far. The sidewalks were packed tighter than subway cars at rush hour; the air smelled like pork fried rust. Vendors were hawking $5 soap bubble guns, and the red and gold Chinese characters plastered on the banks, the Buddhist temple, the fish market, and the retail stores looked like they were about to melt into candle wax.

I stumbled down the pavement, toting a tall kitchen garbage bag that contained a threadbare Armani suit my wife had bought me off the rack at Bergdorf's more than a decade ago. Every few feet,

I'd get stuck behind this little old lady, who'd poke me in the kisser with the tips of her parasol and then holler at me in a voice that sounded like a tunnel full of wind chimes.

I was determined to track down the proprietor of an outfit called the International Tailor Company. I had never laid eyes on the gentleman before; I didn't even know his proper name. All I knew was my wife called him Tom the Tailor and swore he could make a perfect copy of any type garment, including my Armani suit, for a fraction of the price most uptown tailors demand for a custom job.

Maybe you can give me a better reason to go to Chinatown at high noon during a heat wave? If so, I'll bet you haven't priced suits lately. Department store designer suits start around $1,200, and soar toward $3,500 for the fancier labels. Custom suits start around $4,400 at Savile Row–style tailor shops like Leonard Logsdail or Bruce Cameron Clark. Of course, if you really want to shoot the moon, Alan Katzman of Alan Couture can put you in a vicuña and silk custom suit softer than cotton candy for a hefty $30,000.

And yet, the question is—why would anybody even want a suit in this postformal age of dress-down chic and casual Fridays? As G. Bruce Boyer, a respected sartorial scribe and author of *Fred Astaire*

Style (Assouline, 2005), pointed out in an interview, "Suits reached their high point around 1920, and have been going down in popularity ever since."

But then again, as Mr. Boyer hastened to add, with the bursting of the dot-com bubble, custom suits are enjoying a renaissance among both dyed-in-the-wool corporate types and newly minted hip-hop stars who want to dress like grown-ups instead of teenage computer geeks.

"I think guys want individuality in their clothes because they can get it in all other areas of their lives simply by shopping on the Internet," Mr. Boyer said. "They want custom suits in part because they don't have to buy that kind of tailored clothing for the office anymore."

By definition, few things in life can be more individual than a custom suit. Together with your tailor, you pick everything from the fabric to the width of the lapels. You can pad your shoulders, taper your middle, and do whatever else you desire to accommodate your unique physique. The man in the mirror is no longer just another bare naked human, but a knight in white satin linings dressed for success as conqueror of the universe!

Apart from price, there's only one endemic problem with custom suits—the wait. Even allowing for alterations, a department store suit is usually on your back within a week. Custom suits are typically promised in a minimum of six weeks, but often delivered on or around the six-month mark, Mr. Boyer reminded. "Guys are used to getting instant gratification," he noted.

As my wife can attest, I fit that pattern. On the day we marched into Bergdorf's, I had tried on—and taken—the first double-breasted blue Armani size 44 long suit the salesman pulled off the rack. My wife shrieked in dismay. She evidently felt that I had not spent sufficient time examining other blue double-breasted Armani suits in size 44 long. "Women go shopping," I'd informed her with macho pride. "Men go buying."

A decade later, I began to think I might be better off settling for department store threads again because of the unexpected challenges presented by going the custom route, not least the language barrier.

International Tailor had recently moved to a new location at 98 Mott Street. But save for the suite numbers and a sign for "Kenny's Driving School," the building directory was almost entirely in Chinese.

I nodded at two men standing out front. I tugged on the sleeves and the breast pockets of my shirt. I made a scissors clipping gesture with my fingers. Then

I stood at attention as if in front of a fitting room mirror, saying over and over again, "Clothes, suit, tailor." The men shook their heads and answered in Chinese that probably translated into something like, "This guy must be looking for a sex change operation or a prostitute. Let's pretend we don't understand him and maybe he'll go away."

I ventured up the stairs of the building and repeated my pleading pantomimes in vain at a beauty shop, an acupuncturist, and an herbalist reeking with pungent odors. The herbalist closed the door in my face; then he reached for the phone like he was going to call the police or maybe some local "tong" protection gang.

Upon fleeing to the third floor, I breathed a sigh of joy luck relief. There was a sign at the top of the stair that read INTERNATIONAL TAILOR CO. I entered a tiny cubicle crammed with clothes racks and bolts of cloth. A Chinese woman who turned out to be the proprietor's wife sat at a sewing machine in front of a bulletin board stapled with a photo of two handsome young male models in fancy suits standing beside a Mercedes convertible. A short, lean Chinese man in his early sixties entered on my heels.

"Tom the Tailor!" I cried out.

"No, no, Tim!" he exclaimed "Tim Yan! Tim the Tailor!"

My wife surely would have shrieked at the speed with which Mr. Yan and I attended to business. He asked me what kind of fabric I wanted. I pointed to one of the male models in the bulletin board photo who was wearing a tan summer suit. Mr. Yan pulled out a swatch book and flipped to a tan fabric sample labeled "100 percent worsted wool, Made in Italy."

I asked Mr. Yan if he could cut and sew the fabric right there on the premises. He nodded emphatically, then pointed to a framed certificate he had earned from a Hong Kong tailoring organization before coming to New York in the early 1970s. "Nobody study tailor no more," he lamented.

I tried on the Armani suit I wanted Mr. Yan to copy. He made a few quick measurements and suggested some modifications to the pocket flaps and the buttonholes.

"Six hundred twenty dollars," Mr. Yan informed me.

That seemed like a bargain at twice the price. I quickly wrote out a deposit check for $300.

"I have ready in three weeks," Mr. Yan said, frowning at the check. "Next time you come, you bring cash."

I felt like asking why he wanted cash, wondering if maybe he didn't trust a guy like me. But then I figured it was none of my business either way. Besides, I was already imagining that I'd look as cool and crisp, if not as young and handsome, as the male model in the photo when I got my new $620 custom-tailored double-breasted tan suit.

So I just nodded my head at Mr. Yan, a.k.a Tim the Tailor, and slogged back out into the sweltering heat, muttering, "Forget it, Jake—it's Chinatown."

How the King of Bling Saved My Marriage

Five days before my twelfth wedding anniversary, I raced down Park Avenue, gawking at well-heeled passersby and talking to myself out loud like a lunatic. I desperately needed to find a present for my wife, Alison, before it was too late. "Good thing she's no math wizard," I muttered in the direction of a duly startled woman in Manolo pumps, cutoff jeans, and a cowboy hat.

Alison had been telling people that we had been married for thirteen years. I was sure to her it must have seemed at least that long, if not far longer; after all, she'd been married to me the whole time. But she'd also been saying our anniversary was on Saturday, when it was actually on Sunday. As any heartbroken fool who's ever listened to country music knows all too well, twenty-four hours can spell the difference between life and death, marriage and D-I-V-O-R-C-E.

I was hoping against hope that the "King of Bling," Jacob Arabo, might come to my rescue. Mr. Arabo, a.k.a. Jacob the Jeweler, is renowned for selling some of the world's gaudiest and most expensive jewelry to pop, rap, and hip-hop artists like Jay-Z, Beyoncé, Sean Combs, Kanye West, Elton John, Madonna, Mariah Carey, and Ozzy Osbourne—just the crowd my wife keeps begging me to bring home for potluck supper.

I slipped past a pair of muscular men in dark suits and earphones who looked like Secret Service agents, and entered Jacob & Company, a converted brownstone at 48 East 57th Street. Designed to resemble the inside of a diamond mine, the interior walls were covered with sheets of channeled white Corian.

The publicist for Jacob & Company, Thayer Whipple, escorted me to a VIP room in the back of the store equipped with leather armchairs, a bar stocked with adult beverages, and one of the forty-eight flat-screen TVs that have been installed throughout the premises.

Presently, Mr. Arabo, forty, emerged from an adjacent office that featured a see-through aquarium window. With his short curly black hair, sallow complexion, square jaw, and chalk-striped suit, he looked more like a Greek shipping magnate than a Russian Jewish diamond cutter born in Tashkent. But his biography suggested he was always predestined to become the King of Bling.

At age fourteen, Mr. Arabo immigrated to America with his parents and four sisters. Two years later, he enrolled in a jewelry design class; he showed such prodigious skill his teachers urged him to strike out on his own after only four months of formal instruction. In 1981, he opened a jewelry design business in a modest booth in the Diamond Exchange on 47th Street.

In the mid-1990s, Mr. Arabo was discovered by Faith Evans, the R&B singer wife of the late rap star Notorious B.I.G. As Ms. Whipple's press materials noted, "Faith and her husband spawned a sizable buzz throughout the music industry, which resulted in Jacob becoming the go-to guy for jewels." Prior to relocating to 57th Street last December, he had purchased a 75 percent stake in a Swiss watch factory, and formed a partnership with DDM, one of the world's largest diamond suppliers.

I told Mr. Arabo the purpose of my visit. "Don't bring your wife in here," he warned with a wry smile. "It's very dangerous."

Mr. Arabo led me back out to one of the glass-paneled display cases in the front of the store. With the flourish of a character in a James Bond movie, he swiped a magnetic card in front of the panel; the glass lowered. He reached in and grabbed a 22-karat diamond watch with a face measuring 57 millimeters in diameter that featured a multicolored map of the world and separate sets of hands indicating the hour and minute in five different time zones.

"We call this 'The World Is Yours,'" Mr. Arabo said, handing me the watch. "It costs one million dollars. Other jewelers thought I was losing my mind making it, that I'm going to get stuck with it. But already we have sold four of them."

The "World Is Yours" watch was so heavy it almost sprained my wrist. I handed it back, and asked Mr. Arabo if he had something a little less costly in his cases. "Our least expensive watch is $5,600," he informed me.

Mr. Arabo went on to confide that his penchant for designing high-priced, flamboyantly colorful jewelry was inspired by his youthful distaste for the merchandise available back in the Soviet Union. "All the stores sold the same jewelry; it was boring," he said. "That's why I started making my own pieces." Then he added with another wry smile: "Of course, I also like designing simple, elegant jewelry for simple, elegant people."

Back in the VIP room, Mr. Arabo held up a pair of 6-karat diamond earrings, dangling them in front of my eyes. "They look like floating waterdrops, don't they?" he said. I nodded, and asked how much. "Two hundred twenty thousand dollars," he replied.

I confessed that the pieces I'd seen so far were light-years beyond my means. "Just give me a budget then," Mr. Arabo offered. "I will make your wife something you can afford."

"Sure you will," I muttered to myself.

I traipsed out the door and down 57th Street to keep shopping. The moment I entered Tiffany's, I realized that my brief experience with the King of Bling had already spoiled me. The layout of the famous store reminded me of an airport concourse lined with tacky designer boutiques. The craftsmanship of the jewelry seemed downright shoddy compared to Mr. Arabo's. I frowned at a display of Elsa Peretti gold-wire bangles ranging in price from $800 to $1,200. I turned up my nose at Paloma Picasso's "Tanzanite Suite" featuring $17,000 earrings and a $45,000 ring.

I hustled across Fifth Avenue to Van Cleef & Arpels, where I found myself gasping for air inside a dainty little carpeted space furnished like my late great-aunt's living room. A very nice woman in a tan suit showed me a swarm of dragonflies and butterflies made of diamonds, gold, and mother-of-pearl. The prices ranged from $10,000 to $27,500. I politely passed on the bugs and hurried back outside.

Still reeling from seismic sticker shock, I placed a frantic cell phone call to Ms. Whipple, and told her I would take Mr. Arabo up on his offer to design a present for my wife with two stipulations: (1) I needed the merchandise within the next four days, and (2) my budget was $2,000. In effect, I was asking Picasso—in this case, Pablo, not Paloma—to create a masterpiece with a Magic Marker and a bar napkin.

Ms. Whipple hesitated just long enough to make my heart sink. She advised that Mr. Arabo would be happy to work within my modest budget, but he and his wife were flying to Monaco the next evening to attend the annual Red Cross charity ball. "I'll ask if there's something he can do for you before he leaves," she promised.

As it turned out, the King of Bling produced a series of unique creations that spawned both a happy ending—and a potentially expensive new beginning—to my anniversary present pursuit. On the following Sunday morning, Alison awoke to find a white envelope with a gold ribbon lying on her pillow. Inside were two pages of Jacob & Company stationery with pencil drawings of seven different styles of earrings sketched and signed by Mr. Arabo. A note from Ms. Whipple advised that my wife could choose whichever style she wanted. Mr. Arabo would make the earrings upon his return to New York.

"Oh, Bigger, they're beautiful!" Alison exclaimed. "I want all of them."

I told her that would not be possible, at least not this year.

"That's okay," she said with a smile and a kiss on the cheek. "I'll pick one, and then I'll frame Jacob's drawings and hang them on the wall so you'll know what to get me next year."

This Suit Requires a Certain Amount of Finesse

Sometimes you get what's coming to you on this beat. Other times, you've got to go out and get it for yourself. But anytime you catch me humping it back down to Chinatown salivating like a rabid sharpei on a dog day in August just to pick up a custom suit, you can bet it's because some higher power has got me on a short leash with a choke collar.

Sure, I had my own personal reasons for returning to Chinatown. Everybody does. For one thing, I was itching to try on the redesigned Armani knockoff I'd ordered from Tim Yan, a.k.a. Tim the Tailor, exactly four weeks earlier for the almost unbelievably low price of $620.

I was also itching for a variety of ostensibly

unrelated reasons I'll try to put my scratching finger on as we go along. This custom suit caper had already gotten way bigger than me and my size 44 long. Word had come from headquarters that the Boss himself wanted to see how my new threads turned out. Call it good news or bad news. For me, it all boiled down to the same news—my inseams, my street cred, and my wiseacre film noir detective alter ego Jake were on the line once again.

But hey, I got a BlackBerry—was I supposed to text message somebody who cared? Cyber-whining was not in the program. All summer long, the Boss had been sticking up for a pal of mine who's been doing time in the slammer on behalf of the whole organization. I figured the least I could do was give him a first look at my brand-new bespoke. I didn't figure on all the other baggage that would come with it.

I scrambled out of the Canal Street subway under a mess of dark clouds pregnant with rain and existential angst. The air around the Chinese banks, the Buddhist temple, the fish market, and the retail stores steamed with the dank scents of weak tea and wet nylon, but the sidewalks were almost passable. I figured the soap bubble gun vendors and the little old lady who'd kept poking me in the kisser with her parasol the last time around must have fled for shelter from the impending storm.

Armed only with a golf umbrella, I reminded myself that the language barrier had not changed. When I reached 98 Mott Street, the address of Mr. Yan's International Tailor Company, I duly refrained from pulling on the breast pockets of my shirt, making scissors-clipping gestures with my fingers, and standing at attention as if in front of a fitting room mirror, repeatedly saying, "Clothes, suit, tailor."

Instead, I simply waved my golf umbrella at a Chinese man on the stoop. He smiled and nodded, then turned to another Chinese man, chattering in a voice that sounded like crashing cymbals. I reckon his words translated something like, "This guy didn't get the sex change operation he was looking for last month. Now he's come back to stab the acupuncturist and the herbalist."

It was still half an hour before International Tailor Company was scheduled to open, so I went into the Grand Harmony restaurant next door. I found Mr. Yan sitting at a big round table next to his wife, Sheun. "I want call you, but only speak tailor English," he said, leaping to his feet and patting me on the back. "Shoulder, collar, sleeve. You want dim sum?"

One of the waiters hustled past, exclaiming, "Tim the Tailor! Tim the Tailor!"

Mr. Yan picked up a Chinese community newspaper and pointed to a photograph of him. It was the same photograph that had appeared over my *New York Times* column three weeks earlier. He gestured toward a row of Chinese characters that to my ignorant eyes looked like the footprints of a crippled duck.

"You name! You article!" Mr. Yan informed me. "Everybody read! Bring lot of new customer!"

"Maybe you should run for mayor of Chinatown," I said.

Mrs. Yan shook her head from side to side, stabbing at the dim sum crumbs in her mouth with a toothpick.

"No, no, no mayor," Mr. Yan said. "Only make suits."

Mr. Yan led me straight up to his tiny third-floor tailor shop. He carefully laid two garments side by side on the counter. One of them was my old threadbare blue Armani suit. The other was a stunningly beautiful new double-breasted tan suit made of 100 percent Italian worsted wool.

"Armani no good, not professional," Mr. Yan declared, fingering the lapels of both suits. I quickly surmised he was claiming that the boutonnière hole on the Armani model was not as properly spaced as the one he had sewn on my suit.

"Hong Kong master tailor make better collar," Mr. Yan added, plucking a finger full of loose fabric from the collar lining of the Armani. He beckoned me to feel the superior strength and smoothness of my new suit's collar lining. "This collar not ride up in back," he said.

The moment of truth arrived a few moments later when I stood in front of the mirror wearing Mr. Yan's creation. He pointed to a bulletin board photograph of a handsome male model in a tan suit. "Now you look like man in picture," he said.

I wouldn't go half that far, but I could see that my custom suit fit me like my first and last names. The pants were billowy with plenty of break at the cuffs; the coat hung over my shoulders light, loose, and soft as an ocean breeze. I nodded approvingly, and whipped out the $320 cash balance I owed.

Mr. Yan insisted on showering me with gifts, what people on this kind of beat call "swag." First, he gave me a pale green dress shirt and a yellow tie. "Go with suit," he said. Then he gave me a gold ballpoint pen. "You writer," he said. Finally, he gave me a faux diamond-studded watch. "I get it for you from Hong Kong," he said.

I thanked Mr. Yan profusely. Then I packed the suits and the swag in a plastic hanging bag and raced back to headquarters through an afternoon monsoon.

I caught up with the Boss just as he was about to go into a meeting. By that time, I'd been able to duck into a third-floor restroom, take a paper towel shower, and slip back into my new custom threads. The Boss kind of smirked as he gave me the once-over.

"We pay for that suit?" he asked.

I shook my head. Then I took off my suit coat, and invited him to try it on. It was a little big for him, if you know what I mean, but the Boss seemed to like the fabric and the cut. I said I wanted to contribute all the swag I'd gotten from Mr. Yan to the company's Christmas fund for the needy. The Boss sighed and handed back my coat.

"Okay," he allowed. "You've earned your brownie points with the compliance office on this one. At least you get to keep the suit since you paid for it."

I felt like firing off a wiseacre comeback. Instead I just smiled and nodded at the Boss like the guy back on the stoop at 98 Mott Street had smiled and nodded at me. Then I turned away and strode outside.

The rain had stopped, and the setting sun was sparkling like a yellow diamond. But I was still itching to follow this story on from column A to column

Z like the menu in Grand Harmony restaurant. I reached into the pocket of my new custom-tailored pants and pulled out a blue velvet jewelry box, muttering, "Remember, Jake—it's Chinatown."

The Bliss and the Bling Delivered in a Bespoke Suit

If you ever start itching to find some kind of deeper meaning in life, try toting a black plastic hanging bag and a blue velvet box full of rocks custom-made by the King of Bling through the Manhattan subway system at rush hour. I can pretty much guarantee that, within the first couple of stops, some kind of deeper meaning in life will find you.

It caught up with me on a downtown train packed tighter than a Chinatown sidewalk with people whose eyes seemed to bore right through my stain-splotched white pants and all the way into the mysterious bulge inside my right side pocket.

I was hunched over a paperback copy of *The Myth of Sisyphus and Other Essays* by Albert Camus, deliberately not focusing on the fact that the box in my pocket contained the emotionally priceless $2,000 earrings Jacob Arabo, a.k.a. Jacob the Jeweler, had created for my wife's twelfth-anniversary present, or the fact that the black plastic hanging bag contained a suit made exclusively for me by Tim the Tailor in Chinatown.

Instead, I was averting my eyes from the X-ray eyes I felt on me, trying to concentrate on Sisyphus, a guy with whom my wiseacre film noir detective alter ego Jake and I have identified at least since high school, if not since birth.

According to classical mythology, Sisyphus was a cunning, clever mortal who defied the gods and exposed their secrets, kind of like this investigative reporter pal of mine who'd been doing time in the slammer most of the summer. In retribution, the gods cast Sisyphus down to the underworld, where he was forced to roll a rock up a mountain. When the rock reached the top of the mountain, it would roll back down to the bottom, and Sisyphus would have to start all over again.

The ancient Greeks believed that Sisyphus was the world's most miserable man because he was condemned to futile labor for eternity. Existential philosophers like Camus, who believed that all labor is futile, contended that Sisyphus was the world's happiest man because he achieved true consciousness when the rock rolled back down the mountain.

"At each of those moments when he leaves the heights and gradually sinks toward the lairs of the gods, he is superior to his fate," Camus maintained. "He is stronger than his rock."

In rereading Camus's poetic text, I was reminded that Sisyphus was also a married man—and that he and I had a whole lot in common. On the morning of our twelfth anniversary, I had presented Alison with seven original sketches by Mr. Arabo showing earrings he could make within my modest budget. My wife appeared to be momentarily overcome and elated. All she had to do was pick one of the designs.

That's when the rocks started rolling backward.

First, Alison complained that she couldn't pick one design because "they're all so beautiful." A few days later, she reported that she had e-mailed Mr. Arabo a photograph of herself "so he knows my colors and what I look like." A few days after that, she informed me she was going to defer to the judgment of the Jacob & Company staff. Then she gave me one of those looks that said in nonverbal but no uncertain terms that I was missing something, which, of course, I was. At last, she said, "I want you to surprise me."

What a Sisyphean stupid I am! I thought I'd just done that with Mr. Arabo's drawings! But I realized that all my labors had been futile. I was back down at the bottom of the mountain, starting all over again.

When the going gets tough, the tough seek existential enlightenment and a feminine sensibility. I found both in Mr. Arabo's wife, Angela, a comely Uzbek with a halo of curly dark hair and a serene smile. In consultation with her husband and their publicist, Thayer Whipple, she came up with an alternative design for my wife not in the original drawings.

I'm hardly a jewelry connoisseur, but I drew an audible breath when Mrs. Arabo showed me a pair of drop earrings made of 18-karat white gold with centerpieces of 2.07-carat marquis diamonds that seemed to sparkle even brighter than light itself. "We haven't made another pair like it," Mr. Whipple informed me. I stared at the earrings, speechless. Then I wrote out a check for two grand.

"Your wife will be very happy," Mrs. Arabo assured. "If she's not, send her back. One thing about our company, customer satisfaction is guaranteed."

Of course, nothing in life is truly guaranteed. I was

reminded of that fact as I hunched over *The Myth of Sisyphus* in the subway car, contemplating Camus's proposition regarding the influence of a higher power on human affairs, including those of the heart. "Either we are not free and God the all-powerful is responsible for evil," he declared. "Or we are free and responsible, but God is not all-powerful."

Suddenly, a commotion shattered the silence of the subway car. I looked up from the book to see three men and a woman gathered around one of the metal grab poles, snapping their fingers in syncopated rhythm. Instinctively, I dropped my free hand over the velvet jewelry box inside my pants pocket.

Back in my single days, I used to run with an ex-cop who packed heat in an ankle holster; he taught me to replace my lame "Don't mess with me" look with a much more intimidating "Come mess with me" look. Now, inspired by Camus, I affected a look that said perhaps even more matter-of-factly, "It would be futile to mess with me."

The quartet began to sing a hit song by Jackie Wilson, joining in a joyous chorus, "Your love keeps lifting me, keeps on lifting me, keeps on lifting me, higher and higher." Blushing with shame and embarrassment, I whipped out a buck, and handed it to the female member of the quartet. She flashed a double-edged grin, and handed me a business card that identified her group as "A Capella Soul."

Later that evening, I staggered out of the underworld and headed across 23rd Street under a threatening sky to Chelsea Piers where my wife was waiting on a cruise ship a friend of ours had chartered for his fiftieth birthday party. I ducked inside a changing room on the ship and slipped into my new tan double-breasted bespoke from Tim the Tailor. Then I tucked the blue velvet box of rocks from Jacob the Jeweler into my coat pocket and climbed up to the top deck.

I found Alison standing beside a rail on the aft section of the deck, her silhouette framed by the Statue of Liberty and Ellis Island. As I watched her open the box and put on the diamond earrings, I thought about the promise of America and the promise of a marriage.

"Oh, Bigger!" Alison exclaimed, her smile and her new earrings blinding me at the same time. "I love my bling!" She threw her arms around me and kissed me on the lips for one long existential moment.

Then it began to rain and the wind blew hard, rocking the cruise ship, and we had to scatter. If I were a fortune-teller or some kind of genius, I might have recognized it as a harbinger of a far more horrific storm to come. But I was just another husband following his wife back down belowdeck, feeling like Sisyphus and muttering to my wiseacre film noir detective alter ego, "Jake, you think the whole world's turning into Chinatown?"

Act Two

CLOSE SHAVES, CLAY PIGEONS, AND CHÂTEAU BOW-WOW

$1,300 Shoes Beckon and an Unexpected Man Answers

The moon rose over Manhattan at 12:46 A.M. on the last Tuesday in September 2005, and before the clock struck one, I fell head over handcrafted leather heels in love with a pair of shoes. I remember the time and date so precisely because they marked a mystical awakening routinely enjoyed by fashion-conscious women but rarely experienced by sartorially semicomatose men like me.

In retrospect, it's a miracle I can remember anything at all. I was standing in front of the display window of the recently opened Berluti boutique at 971 Madison Avenue, reeling from a series of tequila shots in a nearby cigar bar that had gradually and then all of a sudden decimated my ability to count in Spanish and think in English.

Hey, I had reason to celebrate. After my most recent banishment to Château Bow-Wow, a.k.a. the Doghouse, I had bought a case of Château Lafleur-Gazin 1982 at Zachys's early fall wine auction for just $480. Elated by my newfound bidding prowess, my wife, Alison, had assured me she could sell the wine in her restaurant for at least three times cost.

You might think I'd have the good sense to wait until the auction house actually delivered the Château Lafleur-Gazin before bolting out of Château Bow-Wow to run wild in the streets of La Grande Pomme. But as my long-suffering spouse could attest, good sense was not my style. Then again, neither was falling in love with a pair of shoes.

The same went for most guys I knew in the *Sex and the City* generation. While the Carrie Bradshaws of the world obsess over $2,200 Manolo Blahnik mid-heel alligator halters and $1,150 Jimmy Choo dyed python pumps, my fellow Mister Bigs could have cared less about fashionable footwear. A pair of conservative wingtips, comfy loafers, sturdy winter boots, and a couple of pairs of athletic shoes, each purchased at an average price of $200 or less, were enough to outfit most male closets for decades.

But the shoes in the window of the Berluti boutique were both the simplest and the most elegant ones I'd ever seen. They were made of a single piece of pumpkin-colored leather, shiny and smooth, with only three eyelets and no silly buckles or ostentatious tooling. Indeed, they looked like a "last," the wooden model cobblers carve of a client's feet prior to designing custom shoes.

Later that morning, with the risen sun blinding the moon, I marched through the glass door of the Berluti boutique, only to realize I was entering the sanctum of a worldwide cult. The walls gleamed with a blue-green ocean-sky tint; the shelves and much of the floor were covered with earthy brown leather. In the rear corner, a young Japanese woman in a full-length leather smock was massaging shoes with a linen cloth.

I was greeted by Patrick Ottomani, a forty-six-year-old Frenchman in charge of the retailer's expansion in the United States. Mr. Ottomani advised that the shoes I had my eye on were the "Alessandro" model inspired by the very first style created by the patriarch Alessandro Berluti over a century before. "These shoes are the steps that will take you from where you were to where you are to be," he said with a knowing smile.

I discovered that such spiritually charged sales-manship has always been a trademark of Maison Berluti. A native of Italy originally schooled in wood-working, Alessandro Berluti opened his first boot-making shop in Paris in 1895. After relocating to the Rue Marbeuf just off the Champs-Élysées, Berluti and his heirs made custom footwear for clients rang-ing from Isadora Duncan and the Duke of Windsor to John F. Kennedy and Aristotle Onassis. In 1993, Berluti was acquired by LVMH, a luxury goods con-glomerate with annual sales of over $15 billion.

Berluti now had stores in Paris, London, Tokyo, Milan, Moscow, Hong Kong, Beijing, and New York, but its creative direction still came from Alessandro Berluti's sixty-year old great-granddaughter, Olga Berluti. Ms. Berluti won her initial claim to fame in 1962 when she designed a pair of flat-toed loafers for the artist Andy Warhol. She had since introduced scores of fanciful formal and casual styles, including shoes engraved with the seal of King Louis XV, tat-tooed shoes, pierced shoes, and a "trio" (as opposed to a pair) with matched and unmatched left shoes.

Berluti continued to specialize in making custom shoes that typically required two separate fittings and at least nine months to complete. Bespoke models started at $3,500, and soared as high as the $200,000 an African potentate paid for a pair stitched with white pearls. But ready-made models like the "Alessandro," which started around $1,180, also featured plenty of subtly dazzling natural flaws and tastefully added natural pigments that could be embellished and customized on request.

Ironically, Ms. Berluti was a vegetarian who did not wear leather goods, and yet she saw no contradiction in perpetuating the family franchise with her ethereal approach to footwear. "Show me your feet, show me your shoes, and I will show you who you are," she declared in a transatlantic telephone interview. "The leather was once alive as flesh and blood, and the death of the cow was very violent. Shoes are the last armor of the modern man, and as such they are a very charmed, very physical union of beauty and violence."

Ms. Berluti encouraged clients to treat their shoes with elaborately ritualized tender loving care. In 1992, she founded the Swann Club, named after the protagonist in Marcel Proust's *Remembrance of Things Past*. Swann Club members gathered for black-tie dinners, after which they polished their Berluti shoes with special creams lubricated with drops of champagne. As per Ms. Berluti's recommendation, they also examined and reexamined the pigments and transparencies in the leather under the light of a first-quarter moon.

Berluti sales staff classified and fit clients according to five morphological types: masochistic, pretentious, fragile, disagreeable, and intellectual. With scarcely a hint of disingenuousness, Mr. Ottomani allowed that I was the fifth type. "Some people need heavy, thick-soled shoes to attach themselves to the ground, but you need light, airy shoes because you are a writer," he said. "At the same time, your foot needs to be held because you have a very high arch that requires support."

Mr. Ottomani helped me into a pair of Alessandro shoes, and showed me how to tie the laces in a double-strength Berluti knot. "We can change the color of the shoes anytime, but first you need to get used to them and they need to get used to you," he advised. "So now I want you to go out and start a relationship with your shoes."

I departed the Berluti store, tripping down the sidewalk like the Hunchback of Notre Dame, my neck and shoulders bowed over, my eyes fixed on my new shoes. With each step, I watched the shoes mold to my feet, creating distinctive wrinkles and creases like those on a human face. Then I was struck by a sobering epiphany: I had just paid nearly $1,300 (including tax)—more than twice what I had paid for a custom-made suit in Chinatown—for a single pair of shoes.

I stopped at a sidewalk table in front of Lumi Restaurant, about half a block from the apartment I shared with an investment banker buddy when I was in town. I ordered a double espresso to sober up even further. The moon had already set, but the stars twinkled like dollar signs, chiding me for my extravagance. Just as the espresso arrived, I glanced down and saw several brownish-yellow globs on the soles of my fancy new imported Berluti shoes.

"Ah," the waiter said with a grin as he handed me a napkin, "in France we say that means you will have good luck."

"In America, we say that means I'm headed back to Château Bow-Wow," I replied. Then I picked up my cell phone and called my wife to tell her what I had done.

The Night That Never Happened

There's nothing like being shot at to jump-start an unauthorized night out with the boys. The shots came early and out of left field, and they pretty much obliterated any clear memory of what transpired between a blurry, bloodcurdling moment of dodging bullets and the even blurrier Bloody Mary morning that followed.

It all began innocently enough on a Tuesday night—that much I definitely do remember. I was sitting at a sidewalk café on the Upper East Side wearing a $620 custom-made suit and a pair of brand-new Berluti shoes, a cell phone jammed against my ear. I had just told my wife, Alison, that I'd paid nearly $1,300 for the shoes.

"Oh, Bigger, that's good!" she exclaimed. "You don't do enough things like that for yourself!" There was a pregnant pause. "Now go and have a few more tequilas," my wife said, "and stand in front of a store window on Madison Avenue that has something I want in it."

Silly Sisyphean me, I immediately misinterpreted my wife's words as a green light for the purest of all executive pursuits—the pursuit of fun—at the very next opportunity, which so happened to be the very next night.

In the interests of full disclosure, I'd often stated that I am unapologetically and unequivocally pro-fun, and so, with notable exceptions relating to my own activities, was my wife. That could be risky, especially in New York City. As attested by various edicts of the past two mayoral administrations, including but not limited to the smoking ban and large-scale residential rezoning, the anti-fun forces have been waging a long-running insurgency.

Determined to rally the pro-fun forces, I hopped into a cab and hooked it across town to pick up a venture capitalist buddy I call the V.C., who is very rich, very hyper, and very single. He sauntered out of his apartment building clutching a plastic tumbler filled with vodka.

"I've had a rough week," the V.C. groaned as he slipped into the cab. I noted that it was only Wednesday. He nodded and hoisted his tumbler. "Want some?"

I took a sip, and asked the cabbie to drive us downtown to West Chelsea. It was about half past nine, and the eve was but a first burp. The air was still kind of warm and sultry; the bright lights of the city made the moon and the stars invisible to the naked eye. We were headed to a party courtesy of my pal Rob Gregory, the publisher of *Maxim* magazine, at Spirit nightclub. The party featured the legendary female punk rocker Joan Jett. I told the V.C. that our ostensible business purpose was journalistic research.

"Yeah," he chortled between gulps of vodka. "Right."

"No, man, I'm serious," I said. "Nightlife as we know it is facing a crisis that threatens its very existence."

As I reminded the V.C., that was no laughing matter for the New York City economy. According to a January 2004 report prepared for the New York Nightlife Association, the nightlife industry generated an estimated $9.7 billion in annual economic activity, including $2.6 billion in earnings (primarily wages) and 95,000 jobs. Annual attendance at nightlife spots, the report noted, was over 65 million admissions, more than three times the attendance of all New York City's sports teams combined.

Over the preceding five years, the New York City nightlife industry had developed two increasingly popular epicenters: the Meatpacking District between 14th and 19th Streets and the West Chelsea manufacturing district on 27th and 28th Streets. In those two areas and other nearby pro-fun pockets, there were no less than twenty-two operating establishments that had cabaret licenses and a combined occupational capacity of at least 20,500 people, according to data provided by Anthony Borelli, president of Community Board 4.

To me, all this sounded like a rock-and-rolling good time, but it did not to community leaders like Mr. Borelli, nor to City Hall. Earlier in the year, the city planning board had approved a large-scale rezoning of West Chelsea from manufacturing to mixed-use commercial. That, in turn, had opened the way for the addition of up to two thousand new apartment units the likes of Home Depot and P. C. Richard & Son had already opened stores to capture an anticipated retail boom.

"Nightlife is being pushed out by residential encroachment after the investment of millions of dollars," Robert Bookman, a lawyer for the New York Nightlife Association, complained in a telephone interview. "It's the same story that has been repeated over the years in Soho, Noho, Tribeca, and the Flatiron District."

"We do recognize the importance of the nightlife industry to the city's economy," Mr. Borelli countered in another telephone interview. "But the city is also facing a housing shortage, and a balance has to be struck between the quality of life of residents and nightlife."

Shortly before 10:00 P.M., our cab turned up Tenth Avenue toward West 27th Street. I glanced over at the V.C. He was staring out the window at a darkened ball field near a housing project. Suddenly, his face turned pale.

"Get down!" he hollered.

The V.C. shoved me hard onto the floor of the cab and threw himself on top of me. I heard three shots ring out.

"Step on the gas!" the V.C. ordered our cabbie. "And don't stop!"

I felt the cab speed up and nose over to the left. Then I felt the V.C. pull up from my back. I peeked out the rear window of the cab and saw two men in white T-shirts chasing a third man in a hooded sweatshirt into the darkness off Tenth Avenue.

The V.C. and I jumped out of the cab in front of Spirit on West 27th Street, our veins pumping with adrenaline. Then we slipped into the party and began slamming adult beverages.

Somehow we got separated, and I got swallowed up by a crowd surging toward the stage to join Ms. Jett in a chorus of "I Love Rock and Roll." I blinked my eyes closed.

When I blinked them open again, it was sunrise, and I was hunched over a desk in my wife's former bachelorette apartment on the Upper East Side, clutching a credit card receipt indicating I had spent $387.98 in Bungalow 8, a lounge across the street from Spirit owned by Amy Sacco, the queen of New York nightlife.

A week later, trying to reconstruct the night that never happened in hopes of avoiding yet another banishment to Château Bow-Wow, a.k.a. the Doghouse, I paid Ms. Sacco a visit at her club. We sat down at a banquette I had allegedly occupied a week earlier. I suddenly realized why my credit card receipt had been so high. There were only ten tables in the entire joint, and if you wanted to hold one, you had to order at least one bottle of vodka—which went for $328.37, not including tip.

"You wouldn't be in Château Bow-Wow if you'd gotten hit by the bullets," Ms. Sacco purred in a whiskey-and-cigarettes voice that sounded like Bacall. "But I know how to get you out. We'll send your wife a Bungalow 8 bathrobe."

"Maybe we should throw in a dozen roses," I suggested.

"No, no, the flowers would be too much," Ms. Sacco insisted. "They'd show her you are guilty."

A few hours that seemed like a few minutes later, the bathrobe arrived. "Men don't understand that women want to trust you," Ms. Sacco said. "You don't have to be rich. Once in a while for no reason, without being asked, just pick up the garbage or take her on a romantic weekend. Look at her as a friend. Don't look at her as the enemy who hates you because you left the toilet seat up."

I kissed Ms. Sacco on the cheek. She summoned a six-feet-seven, 300-pound doorman to escort me out to the street. "Put him in a cab," she said. "And make sure he doesn't get shot at this time."

In Search of the Perfect Shave

The gray-haired master barber Boris Mirzakan-dov leaned over and pressed the sharp, steely blade of his straight razor against my throat. My entire face and body went limp. I closed my eyes. Scents of sandalwood, cloves, and black pepper filled my nostrils. I felt the razor scrape a glob of shaving cream from my Adam's apple.

"In the old days," Boris informed me in a thick Uzbek accent, "the barbers perform the circumcisions."

I tried with all my might not to giggle or jiggle, but it was no use. I blinked open my eyes, chortling, and saw Boris lean back and pinch the handle of the razor between his fingers like an artist flourishing a paintbrush.

"I like if people are happy," he said with a wry smile.

I told Boris that we were on the same blade there. I had come to his barber chair in a Midtown Manhattan shop called the Art of Shaving in pursuit of the perfect shave. The timing was not merely coincidental. The week before, I had just barely scraped through two very close shaves of another kind.

The first close shave occurred during an unauthorized night out on the town when a venture capitalist buddy and I were inadvertently caught in a gun battle in front of a West Chelsea housing project. The second occurred when I wrote a newspaper column called "The Night That Never Happened," which detailed the shooting incident and other events that may or may not have ensued at nearby nightclubs.

"There are a lot of things that are missing," my wife, Alison, said when she finished reading my report. Then she glowered at me like she had a pretty good idea of who and what those missing things might be.

Happily, there is nothing like a shave— particularly an old-fashioned straight razor shave— to help you collect your thoughts and other vital appendages. Like death, taxes, and circumcision, shaving is also an inescapable fact of life for most males. American consumers annually spend over $3 billion on shaving and hair removal products, and the average male shaves 20,000 times in his life, according to data compiled by Eric Malka, who founded the Art of Shaving with his wife, Myriam Zaoui.

As every postpubescent male discovers, shaving can be pleasurable and nostalgic, evoking memories of a father teaching his son an eternal art. It can also help attract the opposite sex, while warding off bacteria and germs. But for too many men, shaving is nasty, brutish, and bloody, resulting in nicks, cuts, razor burns, ingrown hairs, and that itchy, irritable feeling that just won't go away.

It was razor burn that inspired Mr. Malka, an entrepreneur, to turn to Ms. Zaoui, a student of Chinese medicine, for a solution. "My wife prepared our first preshave oil product right in the kitchen of our New York apartment," Mr. Malka recalled in a conference call telephone interview from Bal Harbour, Florida. "It is the same product we sell today made of food-grade extra virgin olive oil, castor oil, clove, and black pepper," Ms. Zaoui added.

In 1996, the couple sold their BMW for $12,000 and invested the proceeds in their first store at 141

East 62nd Street. Their stated aim was to enhance the experience of shaving through proper shaving techniques and the use of preshave oils, shaving creams, and aftershave balms made of essential oils used in aromatherapy treatments. "No one was catering to the high-end shaving market," Mr. Malka noted. "Everyone was buying mass-manufactured products."

Touted as the first retail chain totally devoted to men's grooming, the Art of Shaving was apparently carving a lucrative niche. There were stores in Los Angeles, Las Vegas, Atlanta, and suburban Miami, and three in Manhattan. Mr. Malka said he expected to open forty-five more over the next two years. The Art of Shaving products, which included top-of-the-line items like $180 silver-tipped lathering brushes and $250 engraved razors, were also sold over the counter in department stores, including Neiman Marcus, Barneys New York, Saks Fifth Avenue, and Nordstrom.

The Art of Shaving at 373 Madison Avenue where Boris, the master barber, presides was the chain's only Manhattan store offering barbering as well as shaving products. The services menu included a traditional straight razor shave for $35, a traditional shave and a haircut for $80, and a beard and mustache trim for $25. But the featured service was the

"Royal Shave," which combined a traditional shave with an aromatherapy skin treatment for $55.

Boris began my Royal Shave by covering my face with a hot towel to open my pores and warm my beard. After removing the towel, he dabbed a bit of the preshave oil invented by Ms. Zaoui on his fingers, and massaged it into my face. "Every time you shave, you remove a small layer of skin from your face," he noted. "Preshave oil gives added layer of protection to the skin."

Boris applied the first layer of warm shaving cream with a brush made of badger hair. "Synthetic bristles are no good for the face," he said. "Badger is the only animal fur that keeps the lather warm."

Boris razored off the first layer of shaving cream with strokes running with the grain. As he explained, the grain is the direction in which the hairs grow, and as with most men, the grain of my beard pointed downward as far as my Adam's apple, after which it reversed direction and pointed upward.

I closed my eyes again, and asked Boris why he had come to the United States and from where. He said he hailed from the ancient Uzbek town of Samarkand, where he barbered and made fur hats. In 1991, two years after the collapse of the Soviet Union, he and his family joined a mass exodus of over 70,000 Bukharan Jews. "Communication between Muslim people and Jewish people was very bad," he said. "But it is hard to pick up and leave everything you have built up your whole life."

Boris brushed on a second layer of shaving cream, and razored it off with strokes running against the grain. Then he brushed on a third layer of shaving cream, and cleaned up nooks and crannies he missed in the first two passes. I asked him what people talked about in Uzbek barbershops. "Mostly they talk about sex," he replied.

I confided to Boris that some of the events of "The Night That Never Happened" had prompted my wife to consider permanently exiling me to Château Bow-Wow. He placed balls of cotton over my eyes, and sighed, "We see what we can do."

Boris finger-painted my face with an aftershave mask made of rose desert clay infused with rosewater. It was designed to pull impurities out of the skin without hardening like a traditional clay mask. I lay back in the barber chair for a full five minutes feeling more pampered than a supermodel.

Finally, Boris wiped off the aftershave mask with a lemon oil sponge and draped a cold towel over my face. "When you open your eyes, you look fourteen years younger," he promised. Then he removed the towel, applied a moisturizing aftershave balm, and recalculated. "You look ten years younger," he allowed as he popped up the barber chair.

I stared at the mirror, stroking my face. It felt softer and smoother than the honeysuckle lines I'd have to lay on Alison to stay out of Château Bow-Wow. "Better than circumcision," Boris the master barber said, grinning.

I nodded, and handed him a $20 tip. Then I hopped out of the barber chair, promising to return the next week if his Royal Shave did the trick with my wife.

Stalking the Ferocious Clay Pigeon

My wife pointed the business end of a twenty-gauge Browning over-and-under at the pupil of my left eye. The twin muzzles of the shotgun were so close I could smell the cleaning oil. I squinted at the tiny silver sighting bead mounted on the rib above the top barrel. Then I sucked a long hard breath, all of a sudden feeling weak-kneed and squirmy.

Alison raised the stock up from her right armpit. She was wearing a green-quilted shooting jacket, an Hermès scarf, and the kind of look she gives me when she's about to conclude an intramarital argument.

"I like turning clay pigeons into powder," she allowed. "It's very satisfying."

I reckon when your wife wants to shoot a gun, it's best to take her someplace where she can point it at something other than you. That's why I had driven Alison all the way from our home in eastern Long Island to Peace Dale Sporting Clays, a shooting preserve in Wakefield, Rhode Island Now I was having some serious second thoughts that I feared might be my last.

We were standing inside the ramshackle green hut that serves as Peace Dale's office, ammo store, and indoor teaching facility. The proprietor, Richie Frisella Sr., sixty-one, a short, stocky sporting clays champion and renowned instructor, was huddled over Alison's shoulders, helping her aim the Browning at my eyeball.

"We know this gun is empty," Richie Sr. assured, gripping my wife's elbows. "Burn your eyes over the rib."

Alison raised the stock to her right cheek and squeezed the trigger. My body recoiled at the sound of the click, and I staggered backward.

"You got him right dead!" Richie Sr. hollered.

"We know this gun is empty," I muttered, regaining my balance.

"You better stay a good husband," Richie Sr. said, "or it won't be."

Alison lowered the Browning, grinning at me like she knew that settled it and so did I. Even so, Richie Sr. kept us inside the hut for another two hours, taking turns pointing empty shotguns at each other and then swinging the barrels along rows of orange targets nailed to the walls. "This first lesson is about mount and timing," he said.

It was close to sundown when we finally left the hut and climbed into one of the beat-up golf carts Peace Dale uses to ferry people out to the shooting stations. There was a mid-November chill in the air, and the leaves on the trees gleamed like copper plates in the waning light. The kennel dogs were already yelping for supper.

I looked over at Alison and saw her eyes widen with excitement. Along with being a businesswoman and the mother of our eight-year-old son, my wife is one of an estimated 40 million people who enjoy hunting or recreational shooting, according to the National Shooting Sports Foundation. Believe it or not, that's more than all the people who play golf (26 million) and tennis (9.6 million) combined.

Let me hasten to note that Alison does not aim her shotgun at deer, ducks, geese, or other living things, with the notable exception of yours truly. Twenty-three million American gun enthusiasts are target shooters. Roughly nine million of those people, including my wife, participate in sporting clays, a bloodless sport that aims to simulate hunting but with disk-shaped clay pigeons substituted for live game.

Sporting clays is often called "golf with a shotgun." Unlike skeet and trap, in which clay pigeons are released from one or two fixed sites, sporting clays requires the shooter to move along a naturally or artificially landscaped course with anywhere from five to twenty stations. Targets come in three diameters, 60, 100, and 120 millimeters, and they are released in an assortment of trajectories ranging from low-angle "rabbits" that bounce along the ground to high-angle "teals" that rise and fall in parabolic arcs.

Like golf clubs, sporting clays clubs also vary widely in price, exclusivity, and amenities. New York and the New England states boast some of the most highly regarded clubs in the nation. The private Pawling Mountain Club in Pawling, New York, is the sporting clays equivalent of Shinnecock Hills, the private club in Southampton, New York, that has held three U.S. Open golf championships. Addieville Farms East in Mapleville, Rhode Island, which is open to the public, features a bucolic 900-acre layout with overnight accommodations and an executive chef.

Peace Dales, by contrast, is a kind of blue-collar

shrine. Established by Richie Sr.'s father, Edward Frisella, in 1949, the 122-acre preserve is a lopsided doughnut of scrub forests surrounding an abandoned gravel quarry. Like a postapocalyptic film set, the property is littered with rusting pickup trucks and farm implements, tumbledown wooden shacks and target launching towers, and a cherry picker. A round of 100 shots at Peace Dale costs $32 compared with $40 at Addieville Farms East, and lessons are $60 an hour compared with $85 and up at swanky private clubs.

But Peace Dale's humble, slightly unsettling appearance is deceiving, for it also attracts blue-blooded shooters like my wife and our friend Jimmy Gubelman, an architect based in Morristown, New Jersey, who is an avid sportsman. Among the allures are unique and supremely challenging shotgun target games like the Clock, which requires shooters to rotate around a pile of boulders in the abandoned quarry, and the Dirty Thirty, which subjects shooters to a relentless barrage of clay pigeons.

"Peace Dale has the toughest targets anywhere in the country," Jimmy confided in a telephone interview prior to our visit there. "I like to go there right before a competition to sharpen up."

Peace Dale's main attraction, however, is Richie Frisella Sr., the inventor of the Clock and the Dirty

Thirty. Richie Sr. started shooting at age eight, hitting five out eight targets released from an expert trap. He worked the night shift in a local machine shop for eighteen years so he could hunt and train field dogs during the day. When the machine shop closed, he took over management of Peace Dale, which he runs with his wife, Theresa, and son, Richie Jr. Among his competitive sporting clays laurels are a national senior championship and a Rhode Island men's championship.

Richie jerked the golf cart to a stop near a green wooden target control tower that resembled the press box of a small-town high school football stadium. Beyond the tower was a row of shooting stations known as the Five Stand. Alison loaded her over-and-under Browning, and I loaded a twelve-gauge Winchester Model 21 side-by-side my father had given me as a kid back in Texas. Richie Sr. gestured toward the muzzles of our shotgun barrels.

"It's all about connecting the muzzle to the target," he advised. "The muzzle is the most important part of the gun because that where the killing's done."

A second or so later, Richie hollered, "Pull!"

A clay pigeon soared across the Five Stand on a high-arcing left-to-right trajectory. Alison raised the stock of the Browning to her cheek and fired. The clay pigeon exploded in a cloud of orange powder.

"Nice move, young lady," Richie said. He kissed her on the cheek.

We stayed out on the Five Stand for fifty shots each. I figured Alison and I were pretty even most of the way, then I missed two of my last four targets and she hit all four of hers. "Oh, Bigger, I like this!" she exclaimed, grinning again. "It's something we can do together!"

As we climbed back into Richie Sr.'s golf cart with the sun sinking below the copper-colored leaves, I realized there was only one way for me to escape permanent confinement in Château Bow-Wow, a.k.a. the Doghouse—I was going to have to connect my muzzle to some sporting clays targets and shoot my way out.

Act Three

YIN, YANG, BUCKING, AND BRANDY

Is Anybody Necessary? Dr. Ying and the Four Noble Truths

I seem to start every year trying to reexamine what is real and what is not, and it just about always gets me into a deep heap of existential trouble. One definition of insanity is doing the same thing over and over and expecting a different result. But what do you call it if you do the same thing over and over and keep getting different results? Is that sanity?

And what do you call it when cancer kills two close friends and that hits you a whole lot harder than the fact that tens of thousands of people you don't know were killed in wars around the world? Is that just tough luck? Or just more of the same old life and death?

Those were the kinds of sumo wrestler-sized thoughts that were strangling my mind as I staggered toward the Mahayana Buddhist Temple in Chinatown during a driving rain. It was the Thursday before New Year's Eve 2006. I was hoping to get a couple of days jump on my annual reality reexamination ritual—and maybe make a few quick bucks for a change.

After a series of expensive hedonistic executive pursuits, I was on a low-budget intellectual pursuit. My official mission was to seek answers to a question inspired by *New York Times* columnist Maureen Dowd's bestselling book, *Are Men Necessary?* For me, that provocative question begged the corresponding question, "Are women necessary?" which, in turn, begged the even larger question, "Is anybody necessary?"

But the sight of the Mahayana Buddhist Temple threw me for an unexpected philosophical loop that taunted my ability to distinguish between what was real and what was not. The temple was housed in a red and yellow box-shaped building nestled between the colonnaded archway of the Manhattan Bridge and a booth that sold $15 bus tickets to Boston. A pair of faux gold-painted lions that could have come straight from a Hollywood back lot guarded the plateglass front doors.

I ducked under an overhang, shaking off my black umbrella, and silently reviewed the steps that led to this strange rain-soaked juncture. I had begun my intellectual pursuit by consulting experts in Western thought. But when I telephoned a philosophy professor at Harvard, my alma mater, he brusquely informed me that he would have nothing to contribute. Fuming, I contacted Shelly Kagan, Clark Professor of Philosophy at archrival Yale University, who pointed out a logical flaw in my approach.

"You can ask are men necessary or are women necessary, but when you ask if anybody's necessary, you're shifting meaning," Dr. Kagan said. "Are people necessary to the happiness of other people? The answer has to be yes. If there are no people, then there are no people to be happy or unhappy."

Dr. Kagan said that my big question, properly rephrased, ultimately concerned the meaning of life. "The truth is very complicated and doesn't easily boil down to one sentence," he allowed. "I don't have a short essay on the meaning of life."

Instead, Dr. Kagan graciously referred me to the next best thing. It was a 262-page paperback book by Princeton University professor Peter Singer entitled, *How Are We to Live?* After surveying the evolution of philosophical thought from Socrates to

Betty Friedan, Dr. Singer concluded that people ought to "take the point of view of the universe" when making moral judgments about how to live their lives.

I'm no moral philosopher, but that sure seemed like a logical flaw to me. How could any man or woman take "the point of view of the universe" other than through an act of extraterrestrial projection, a mind-out-of-body flight from planet Earth into outer space? Even Dr. Singer conceded: "This is not a phrase to be taken literally, for unless we are pantheists, the universe itself cannot have a point of view at all."

My own point of view became further disoriented when I slipped between the lions in front of the Mahayana Buddhist Temple, and entered the lobby, inhaling the sweet-and-sour smell of incense.

On the left, a gift shop counter displayed beaded jewelry and ceramic statues. On the right, a mud-splattered carpet led to a cavernous semidarkened room humming with a piped-in Chinese chant. A faux gold Buddha that must have been at least ten feet tall peered down from an altar bedecked with apples and oranges.

Presently, a Chinese man strode into the lobby wearing a gray NYPD sweatshirt, khaki pants, and white jogging shoes. "Hello, my name is Dr. Nelson Ying," he said. "Welcome."

Dr. Ying ushered me into a lounge separated from the giant Buddha by a glass partition. An assistant arrived with paper cups of green tea. I asked Dr. Ying if he was a lama, one of the terms designating a Buddhist holy man.

"I've been called an ass, but never a lama," he replied, grinning, and then adding, "Actually, I have a PhD in nuclear physics, and I am an adjunct professor at the University of Central Florida in Orlando."

Dr. Ying told me that he and his parents had fled Shanghai in 1955, six years after the Communist takeover. Arriving in New York with only $600, his father, James Ying, opened a chain of gift shops that grew from Chinatown into the suburbs. Meanwhile, his mother, Annie Ying, established the first storefront Buddhist temples on the East Coast, and a rural retreat in upstate New York. In 1995, she founded the Mahayana Buddhist Temple at 133 Canal Street.

"I was the first Buddhist preacher licensed in the state of New York to perform Buddhist weddings, but I am not a priest," Dr. Ying informed me. "Priests cannot kill animals, and therefore must remain vegetarians. Also, they are not allowed to marry."

Dr. Ying paused to take a sip of green tea. "I was married to my first wife, Barbara, who died," he confided. "I am now married to my second wife whose name is Patricia. I drink alcohol, but not to excess, and I try not to waste anything. I certainly do not waste the emotions of my wife by being unfaithful to her."

Not wanting to waste Dr. Ying's time, I quickly explained how my intellectual pursuit had taken some unexpected turns, leaving me dazed and confused by a metaphorical downpour of logical flaws and philosophical red herrings.

"Perhaps you have come to the right place," Dr. Ying said, nodding sympathetically. "I call Buddhism the Red Cross of religions. It is based on what we call the Four Noble Truths: that there are sufferings in the world; that the sufferings have a cause; that the sufferings can be ended; and that there is a methodology for ending them we call the Eightfold Path."

I pulled a dog-eared copy of Dr. Singer's book from my raincoat. Dr. Ying stared at *How Are We to Live?* for what seemed like an eternity.

"My answer is a sample of one," he said at last. "What do I do? I find joy in helping others. But I am careful to take the middle path. If I ignore a person who is suffering, he may perish. But if I help them from cradle to grave, they merely have a crutch. I try to develop a master-student relationship in which the student becomes the master. As Lee Ann Womack says, 'Don't let a helping heart leave you bitter.' "

I gulped down my green tea, and bowed to Dr. Ying, thanking him. Then I bowed to the faux gold giant Buddha, and staggered back out into the pouring rain.

As I passed the gold-painted lions in front of the temple, I asked myself one final philosophical question: What could be more real—or more necessary—than the lay preacher of an Eastern religion who had a Ph.D. in nuclear physics and the wisdom and humility to quote the lyrics of a country-and-western singer?

A Career, Briefly, in Polo

I swung into the saddle above a chestnut gelding named C.X., knowing I was about to bet my house—and maybe my life—on the outcome of a polo match at Cyprus Creek Farm near Wellington, Florida. A groom offered up a borrowed polo mallet. I clutched the double reins with my left hand and grabbed the mallet with my right, hoisting the hitting end above my polo helmet like a spear.

Chris Delgatto, thirty-five, a founder of a national firm based in Manhattan that buys estate jewelry, sidled next to me on a chestnut mare. We were dressed in the ad hoc uniform of our Blue Team, jeans and blue sweaters. But he was wearing a pair of fancy riding boots made in Argentina and a giddy-up grin. I was wearing beat-up cowboy boots and a frown masking unadulterated fear.

"Feel like a knight going off to battle?" Chris asked.

"I feel like I ought to have my head examined," I said.

"That's why polo is such a fraternity," Chris replied. "We all know we're a little off our rockers. But even the pros respect you because they know you're out there doing something dangerous. You're on a 1,200 pound animal galloping at speeds up to 30 miles an hour."

We kneed our horses and walked them down a dirt road, our nostrils filling with the sharp dry smell of leather and the sweet wet scents of pine and palmetto. There were wooden-fence paddocks on either side of the road, a couple of horse trailers and a mobile home, and beyond them the grassy expanse of a regulation outdoor polo field 300 yards long and 160 yards wide.

Chris Briere, forty-five, the resident pro at Cyprus Creek Farm and the captain of our Blue Team, rode over on a bay gelding. "I've got one last piece of advice," Captain Briere said to me. "Tuck and roll. When you go down, don't stick out a limb."

I nodded and spit at the ground. Then my head

Trying on my new custom suit at Tim the Tailor's shop in Chinatown. (Courtesy of G. Paul Burnett for *The New York Times*)

Jacob "The Jeweler" Arabo's sketches saved both my behind and my marriage. (Courtesy of Tony Cenicola for *The New York Times*)

There's nothing like the real thing when it's Jacob "The Jeweler's" earrings. (Courtesy of Don Hogan Charles for *The New York Times*)

The Berluti shoes I fell toe over heels in love with. (Courtesy of Ruby Washington for *The New York Times*)

Dad polo-horsing around in front of Harrison and his mother. (Courtesy of Marc Serota for *The New York Times*)

Smile and be nice when your wife proves she's a crack shot at sporting clays. (Courtesy of Richie Friscella, Sr.)

Airborne with Lee Lauderback
in the TF-51. (Courtesy of Stallion 51)

I'm thumb-up for takeoff in the cockpit of a TF-51. (Courtesy of Stallion 51)

484745

You can't go wrong in a thong—or can you?

The mighty Harrison Hurt at bat in a Sag Harbor Little League game. (Courtesy of Gordon Grant for *The New York Times*)

Under center with the New York Jets—"Set! Hut!" (Courtesy of Robert Caplin for *The New York Times*)

Former New York Jets defensive lineman Dewayne Robertson gives me the shakes. (Courtesy of Robert Caplin for *The New York Times*)

Working out with Charles Askegaard and the New York City Ballet company. (Courtesy of Sara Krulwich for *The New York Times*)

In hair and makeup room, George Lopez promises to make me a TV star.
(Courtesy of Jamie Rector for *The New York Times*)

A TV star is born...(Courtesy of Jamie Rector for *The New York Times*)

... and then born again. (Courtesy of Jamie Rector for *The New York Times*)

"Getchur red-hawt hawt dawgs!" at Shea Stadium with the New York Mets. (Courtesy of Joe Fornabaio for *The New York Times)*

Getting nailed at the Coney Island Sideshow School. (Courtesy of Julien Jourdes for *The New York Times*)

Eating fire is hot stuff. (Courtesy of Julien Jourdes for *The New York Times*)

Paddling toward disaster and deliverance on the Nantahala River. (Courtesy of Steve Dixon for *The New York Times*)

started spinning as I remembered the series of coincidences that led me to choose polo as my latest—and possibly, last—executive pursuit.

It all began with an article I wrote for the Sunday Business section of *The New York Times* in August 2004. In it, I explained how to get started in the so-called sport of kings at the Southampton Hunt and Polo Club on eastern Long Island for the relatively modest investment of $2,000. Chris Delgatto had read the piece, and taken the bait.

"I was working twenty-hour days to build my company," he recalled. "It was invigorating, but I realized that if I kept working like that it would be too much. The people around me were pushing me to do something, to try a sport or a hobby. When I saw your article, I realized polo was something I could connect with."

Polo also jibed with Chris's business ambitions. In 1998, he and two partners founded a company called SellJewelry, which he described as a national firm specializing in buying jewelry from the public and reselling it to collectors. Having established offices in New York, Chicago, San Francisco, and Palm Beach, he had recently changed the name of his company to Circa as part of an effort to go more upscale. "The polo demographic is our demographic," he noted.

What amazed me was how quickly Chris had taken to the saddle. He told me the only horses he had ridden before the fall of 2004 were on the merry-go-round at Coney Island. The first time I saw him ride was in an indoor polo arena in Bridgehampton the following January. Although he had been playing polo for less than six months, he looked like he was born in the stirrups with mallet in hand.

Last summer, Chris rented my house in Sag Harbor, just a few miles from the Southampton Hunt and Polo Club. He quickly progressed from minus 2 goals, the rookie ranking, to minus 1 goals of a possible plus 10, the highest ranking. This year he was wintering in Florida with other Southampton club players and starting a polo team under the sponsorship of his jewelry company. "It's just addicting," he confided.

If I was partly responsible for Chris's infatuation with polo, I felt no guilt or remorse. Rather, I was impressed, envious, and intrigued. In a sense, we had switched lives. He had literally moved into my own home and risked his life acting on my words. Now he was daring me to emulate his derring-do by joining him in a polo match.

I should have known better than to accept the challenge. I was just a drugstore cowboy. In 1975, I had played two of the six seven-minute chukkers, or periods, in a polo match to research an article for *Texas Monthly*. I had vowed at the time that if I survived, I would never tempt fate like that again.

Thirty-one years later, I was evidently suffering a simultaneous attack of memory loss and the middle-age crazies. Worse, I was also experiencing a middle-class financial pinch. I needed to rent my Sag Harbor house again this coming summer to make ends meet. I figured if I played a chukker of polo with Chris, he would feel obligated to ante up for another summer rental—especially in the not unlikely event that I broke my neck.

The longest seven minutes of my life began with a jolt and a blur of color. Chris and I had just ridden out to midfield to join the fourth member of our Blue Team, a former investment banker named Ali Bailey. The White Team, which consisted of four Southampton Hunt and Polo Club members led by a Brazilian-born commodities trader, Marcello Dorea, turned their mounts to face ours.

Suddenly, Captain Briere threw down a white polo ball, and the match was on. C.X. bolted after the pack in a bone-jarring canter. Somehow I managed to rein him in about twenty yards in front of the White Team goal posts. The game slowed for my benefit, and Ali hit the ball toward me. I swung my mallet, and whiffed. Ali rode in behind me, and nudged the ball again. I took another swing, and saw the ball skid forward. Chris whacked it into the goal.

"Nice assist!" he cried out.

Captain Briere threw the ball in once again, and once again, C.X. bolted. But this time he was bobbing his head and bucking his rump, straining at the bit like he was going to go ahead and play the game even if I couldn't. My butt slammed against the saddle ten times in a row. My vertebrae compressed like worn-out shock absorbers. A sharp pain shot through my ribs. I felt like C.X. had hammered me into a corset of nail-bearing two-by-fours.

"Whoa, boy!" I hollered, leaning back in the saddle.

C.X. pulled up, sneezing. I sucked a few deep breaths and then spurred him into a canter. My back immediately seized up again. I jerked the reins and made C.X. walk. We wandered aimlessly around midfield with him sneezing and me wincing until Captain Briere called the end of the chukker.

When we dismounted, the White Team captain Marcello Dorea graciously welcomed me to the polo fraternity. "That took some real guts on your part," he said. "The horses are too fresh, too jumpy because they've been on hiatus since October. A lot of players won't even ride them this early in the season."

"Now you tell me," I groaned.

Chris Delgatto strode up, flashing his giddy-up grin and assuring me that my reckless show of bravado had not been in vain. "I definitely want to rent your house again this summer," he said, hugging me.

Overcome with joy, I realized that polo and pain had a lot in common—they both made you feel so alive even though you sometimes wished you were dead.

Yin, Yang, and Back Relief at 105 Degrees

I never thought I'd find myself standing on one leg in a mirrored room heated to 105 degrees, staring in the general direction of the invisible "third eye" supposedly located on my forehead while pretending to be a tree. But then again, I never thought I'd be reckless enough to bust my back riding a polo pony for the first time in thirty years. Funny how the old yin tries to reconnect with the young yang when the executive pursuit of pleasure becomes a pursuit of pain relief at all costs.

Of course, I knew from the moment I entered the Zebra Yoga studio in my adopted hometown, Sag Harbor, New York, that I wasn't supposed to think at all. I was supposed to clear my brain of noise and imagery. Allow my mind and body to become one.

Just let it go. But I couldn't let it go—not with the reflection of my chimerical evil twin, Larry, smirking at my every awkward move.

Stripped down to identical black bathing suits and white T-shirts, Larry and I looked like sweat-soaked, slow-breathing, spitting images of each other. But there was a critical difference in focus. Instead of staring at his third eye, Larry kept glancing over at the reflection of the yoga teacher, Lienette Crafoord.

A strawberry blonde with robin's-egg eyes and an athletic figure wrapped in black spandex, Lienette prowled the floor like a self-enlightened lioness, offering an uninterrupted stream of yoga instruction.

"You're standing tall and proud, reaching to the ceiling," she purred. "You're inhaling and exhaling through your nose. Your mind is clear. Your mouth is closed. Your face is relaxed . . ."

I squinted at my own reflection, trying again to clear my mind, but it was no use. I kept thinking about how Larry had led me to yoga in a classic case of doing the right deed for all the wrong reasons. It all started the previous Saturday when we joined Lienette and a crowd of local businesspeople at the Sag Harbor Village Ladies Improvement Society's annual fund-raising ball. Next thing I knew, Larry made his move, preceding me like a bad reputation.

"You have this glow about you," he told Lienette as if it were just a matter of fact, extending his right hand and then introducing himself by my name.

"A lot of people notice it," Lienette returned, grasping his outstretched hand. "A lot of people want a part of that. That's why they come try yoga."

Larry barreled through that opening quicker than you can say Buddha, affecting the air of a high-rolling corporate executive and putting foot in mouth when he should have had tongue in cheek. "Just hurt myself real bad playing polo down in Palm Beach," he said, groaning and twisting his torso from side to side "Early in the season, horses were too fresh. Like riding jackhammers."

Larry grabbed the bar rail, arching his back. "Brand-new Ferrari Modena stalled twice on the way back to the boat," he continued. "Canceled the sail to Lyford Cay, jumped right in the hot tub. Thank God, I had the corporate jet that weekend. Never would have made it flying commercial."

Lienette just kept glowing her glow and smiling a blissful smile, as though she could see right through to Larry's lying soul and it didn't faze her at all.

"Many people come to yoga because of injury," she said. "Then they discover it's not just physical. There are all these opportunities for emotional and spiritual healing. Suddenly, having come for an injury, they go on a journey of self-discovery."

Larry immediately signed us up for sessions at Lienette's studio, leaving me, as usual, to do the due diligence. I quickly discovered that there were about as many kinds of yoga as there were words in the *Kama Sutra*. Indeed, yoga had undergone an explosion of popularity over the last decade with an estimated 15 million people in the United States practicing traditional disciplines like Astanga, Iyengar, and Vinyasa, and innumerable New Age variations.

Lienette taught Bikram yoga, also called "hot" yoga. It was invented in 1974 in Beverly Hills by Bikram Choudhury, a three-time national yoga champion from India. It consists of twenty-six poses performed in an indoor space heated to over 100 degrees, the equivalent of working out in a sauna. According to the Bikram Web site, the heat enhances the healing of chronic injuries by enabling you to "work deeper into your muscles, tendons, and ligaments to change your body from the inside out."

Once disparaged as a Hollywood fad, Bikram yoga has attracted numerous celebrity followers over more than thirty years. But entertainment industry students like Shirley MacLaine, Raquel Welch, and Quincy Jones have recently been joined by former world-class athletes like John McEnroe and Kareem Abdul-Jabbar, and by the conditioning coach of the Seattle Seahawks football team, who prescribed it not only for injured players but also for those seeking an edge in flexibility and endurance.

A former triathlete and professional sailor, Lienette had turned to hot yoga to heal a nagging hip ailment. Amazed by the overnight results, she went on to study with Bikram Choudhury for nine weeks in Beverly Hills to become certified as an instructor. After consulting at various studios for four years, she moved to Sag Harbor to become the operating partner in Zebra Yoga. Her classes cost only $20, and they attracted lawyers, bankers, real estate executives, and entrepreneurs looking to relieve workday stress, as well as "weekend warriors" hoping to heal sports injuries.

"I'm a yogi, you're a yogi," Lienette said when Larry and I arrived. "If you're practicing the connection between mind and body, you're a yogi."

The only yogis I knew had the last names Bear and Berra, but I figured this might be my last legal hope for lasting pain relief. I had learned on a visit to a local chiropractor that my borrowed polo pony had pounded my L5 vertebra, sending my iliocostalis and quadratus muscles into spasms. After massaging me with electrical current, the chiropractor had adjusted—make that yanked—my back so violently, I felt as if I'd been hit by a truck.

It took me only one ninety-minute session to realize that Bikram yoga was not for wimps, either. Lienette guided us through fifty-five minutes of standing poses with names like Half Moon, Standing Bow and Awkward Pose, which demanded that you do a knee bend perched on your toes. I stumbled and wobbled a lot more than I posed, straining muscles I never knew I had and feeling like a doddering fool. Larry's reflection kept smirking at me in the mirrors.

We then spent thirty-five minutes on the mats, twisting ourselves into human pretzels. I was supposedly striving for a "tourniquet effect" by compressing my organs into the postures, then releasing the postures to flush my organs with oxygenated blood. But my beleaguered system seemed to flush only sweat, tears, and malodorous bile. "There are a lot of toxins coming up," Lienette allowed, "especially when you've been injured."

By the end of the session, I felt as if I'd been run over by another truck. I spent the rest of the evening in bed practicing Savasana, the so-called Dead Body pose. Larry ran off to a local pub, purportedly to lubricate his system.

But when I awoke the next morning, I was stunned.

My old yin had reconnected to my young yang. I rolled out of the sack without crippling back pain for the first time in over a week. Elated, I rushed over to Zebra Yoga for a second session.

Upon entering the studio, I saw Larry's reflection in the wall mirrors. I immediately disclaimed him and all his misbehavior. "You are whole and perfect just as you are," Lienette said. "Nothing should be stealing your peace."

Moments later, Lienette guided me into a Half Moon. I stole a glance at the wall mirrors—almost all of my back pain had miraculously disappeared, and so had Larry's reflection.

No Stranger to Fine Cognacs

A winter wind sliced through the sidewalks of Tribeca like a giant razor blade, chafing my cheeks and piercing all the way to my spine. I hiked up the collar of my overcoat, walking faster. My wife and son had just taken a flight to a Central American resort. Left alone to labor in gloom, I was hoping to take the edge off the cold dark night even as the words of my existential philosopher hero, Albert Camus, rattled my brain.

"There comes a moment when the creation ceases to be taken tragically; it is merely taken seriously," Camus observed in *The Myth of Sisyphus*. "Then man is concerned with hope. But that is not his business. His business is to turn away from subterfuge."

I ducked inside the Brandy Library at 25 North Moore Street. It was a classy-looking joint with amber lighting, overstuffed leather chairs, and wood-paneled walls. The shelves were stocked with over a thousand bottles of so-called brown spirits—i.e., brandy, scotch, and bourbon—complemented by a few dozen books. I sat down at a bar covered with mosaic glass tiles, where I was greeted by the spirits sommelier, Ethan Kelley.

A voluble, knowledgeable man in white shirtsleeves and old-fashioned suspenders, Ethan suggested that I should consider a kind of escapist "flight." By that, he meant what brown spirits connoisseurs call a flight, a tasting sample comprising eight shot glasses. More specifically, he recommended a flight featuring eight of the world's finest Cognacs. "Giving this kind of advice is my sole purpose in life," Ethan assured.

I might as well have been thrown into the pro-verbial Briar Patch. I love Cognacs right next to my aforementioned spouse and child. I'm no wine snob; I can't even remember how to spell oenologist with-out a dictionary. But I confess to be pretty picky about Cognacs, which I always spell with a capital "C" in honor of the region in southwestern France from whence they come.

As I told Ethan, my preferences were formed a decade ago on a trip my wife and I took to Cognac to stock up for her restaurant. I quickly learned that Cognacs are a type of brandy, but not all brandies are Cognacs. True Cognacs must come from Cognac and nowhere else. Most Cognacs are made with wine from either Ugni blanc or Colombard grapes, which must be distilled twice in copper pots and aged at least two and a half years in oak casks.

While the age of a Cognac is an important deter-minant of quality, both producers and connoisseurs admit that the widely used letter rankings are really just marketing tools. "Very Special" (V.S.) Cognacs are aged up to three years. "Very Special Old Pale" (V.S.O.P.) Cognacs are aged at least four years. "Extra Old" (X.O.) and "Napoleon" denote the highest grades. To qualify as an X.O. or a Napoleon, a Cognac must be aged a minimum of seven years, but that leaves a lot of room for variations in quality since these umbrella categories include Cognacs aged as long as sixty years as well as Cognacs aged only ten years.

For more than a century, the Cognac industry has been dominated by the Big Four: Martell, Rémy Martin, Courvoisier, and Hennessey. Together, the Big Four account for more than 90 percent of the Cognacs consumed in America. Most of these Co-gnacs are blends, with 50 percent of the mix coming

from the centrally located Grand Champagne subre-
gion (not to be confused with the Champagne region
farther north) and the rest from outlying subregions.

Over the last twenty years, however, independent
single-grape Cognac producers have enjoyed a resur-
gence. If the Big Four Cognacs are the rough equivalent of blended scotches, single-grape Cognacs are
the equivalent of single-malt scotches. Independents
like Gabriel & Andreu, which also owns the Pierre
Ferand brand, offer Cognacs made entirely from
Grand Champagne, Petit Champagne, Borderies, or
Fin Bois grapes. The only blending involved is mixing
Cognacs of different ages, say a sixty-year-old Grand
Champagne with a ten-year-old Grand Champagne.

America reigns as the leading importer of Cognac,
consuming over 49 million bottles annually, or 42
percent of worldwide sales, according to a 2004
study by the Trade Environment Database, a research
project under the auspices of American University.
Europe ranks second with a 40 percent market share,
and Asia is third with 18 percent. Although worldwide sales slumped nearly 15 percent in the wake of
the 1997 Asian financial crisis, sales in the United
States have more than tripled in the last decade.

"Interestingly enough, one of the reasons for this
momentum is Cognac's new and fast-expanding mar-

ket in the mainstream hip-hop urban culture," the study noted. "Different types of Cognac brands, including Rémy Martin, Hennessey, and Courvoisier, have been benefiting from exposure to pop-hit music videos with rap stars like Eminem, Busta Rhymes, and others."

I reckoned the rappers must have had out-of-town gigs the night I visited the Brandy Library. Most of the customers were Wall Street types in their thirties and forties. But Ethan insisted that the influence of a youthful demographic was increasing. "Since we opened a year and a half ago, our top sellers have been scotches, but Cognacs sales are steadily going upward, especially among customers under thirty," he said. "We're seeing people turning away from their vodka sodas and attempting to do something more stylish."

Of course, the Cognacs on the Brandy Library menu were considerably more expensive than other spirits. The lowest-priced Cognac was a Gabriel & Andreu Fin Bois listed at $10 a glass. The highest-priced Cognacs were a Rémy Louis XIII listed at $162 a glass, a Pierre Ferand Ancestrale at $182 a glass, and a Pierre Ferand 1914 at $230 a glass. By comparison, the most expense single-malt scotch was a thirty-year-old Macallan at $135 a glass.

The flight of X.O. Cognacs Ethan chose for me to

sample was a relative bargain at only $48. It arrived on a stylish silver tray covered with a paper doily identifying the contents of the eight shot glasses. The selection essentially pitted one of the Big Four, a Hennessey, against seven Cognacs made by independent producers, a Marquis de Gensac, a Frapin, a Prunier, a Delamain Pale and Dry, a Camus Borderies, an Otard, and a Fronsac.

This was tough and potentially dangerous work, but I figured if someone had to do it, then it might as well be me. I began our ad hoc Cognac taste test by taking a small sip from each glass in order from the first to the eighth. In round two, I did some comparison sipping under Ethan's guidance, paying special attention to the "finish," or lingering aftertaste, of each Cognac. Round three was the medal round in which I declared my preferences.

If I was the guaranteed winner, the stand-in for the Big Four claimed the boobie prize. By the end of round three, I had drained every drop from every glass save for the Hennessey glass, which remained one-third full. "The Hennessey's heavy in body, and almost a little unbalanced, like a cabernet with all the tannins but no berry rush," Ethan noted. "It's reminiscent of a bad candy bar."

No doubt because of my philosophical biases, I

gave the highest marks to the single-grape Camus Borderies. "It comes from a region that often gets ignored, but it's done well and aged well," Ethan said approvingly. "And the finish? It's one of the most extraordinary and most floral, with hints of lavender and violet."

A few minutes later, I staggered back out on the sidewalks of Tribeca. I still missed my wife and son, and hoped they would come home safe and soon. But with the warmth of a flight of Cognacs rising from my belly to my soul, I felt like I could turn away from subterfuge and head fearlessly into the razor-bladed wind.

Act Four

FLIGHTS OF FANCY AND FATHERHOOD

Gaining Altitude, Doubts in Tow

I hunkered in the rear cockpit of a World War II vintage airplane named Crazy Horse, my heart throbbing with awe and anxiety. I had a blue Kevlar crash helmet on my head, a boom mike in front of my lips, and a parachute strapped to my back. As I stared out at the sun-drenched tarmac of Kissimmee Gateway Airport, a soft central Florida breeze bussed my cheeks. I wondered if it was the kiss of death.

"Harry, you ready to do this?"

The voice of Lee Lauderback, a square-jawed fifty-five-year-old veteran pilot, crackled over the intercom from the forward cockpit.

"Ready, Captain," I replied in a baritone full of bravado. "Let's go."

Lee and I were in a TF-51 Mustang, the dual-control flight trainer version of the single-seat P-51 Mustang, one of the most illustrious propeller-driven fighter planes in American history. With its sleek silver fuselage, blue conical nose, and 1,700-horsepower Merlin engine designed by Rolls-Royce, our Mustang could fly almost 500 miles an hour and climb to an altitude of over 41,000 feet.

I glanced at the antique instrument panel, tightening my four-point safety harness. The Mustang's jet-like capabilities were all the more remarkable given that this particular plane was built in 1944. Several of its interior rivets were ringed with what I surmised to be mid-twentieth-century dust.

"All right," Lee announced. "If you're clear of the canopy rails, I'm gonna roll it forward—don't want to mess up your hair—and we'll go ahead and wake up the Merlin."

The Mustang's engine erupted with a pop, a cackle, and a plume of white smoke. The propeller spun so fast I could see right through the blades and all the way up into the wild blue yonder. We were still on the ground, and I still had time to call it quits. But I prayed for the guts to hang in like my dearly departed daddy would have done.

I reckoned this might very well be the ultimate

executive pursuit. There are scores of fantasy sports camps where you can test your mettle against professionals. There are driving schools where you can learn to race a car like a bat out of hell. But with the possible exceptions of skydiving or jumping off the Brooklyn Bridge without a bungee cord, I could think of nothing that even came close to the gravity-defying exhilaration of flying a TF-51 Mustang—or offered such unbeatable bragging rights—especially if you'd had absolutely no previous piloting experience.

My preflight briefing had begun at 0900 hours when I arrived at Stallion 51, the private flight operations company Lee runs from a cluster of hangars a few miles from Walt Disney World. Lee led me into a conference room equipped with a whiteboard, a video screen, and two model airplanes. I mentioned that my father had been a so-called ninety-day wonder, a moniker given to men who learned to fly World War II fighters at the Naval Air Station in Pensacola in only three months.

Lee promised to make me a less-than-ninety-minute wonder. After barely over an hour of ground training, we were going on a sortie in the TF-51 Mustang. But this wasn't going to be just a joy ride. According to Lee, I was going to do about 95 percent of the flying. "We're going to let you drink the Kool-Aid," he said. "You're going to have the total immersion experience."

I gulped bottled water as Lee recounted his background and the genesis of Stallion 51. Raised in Orlando, he started flying at age fourteen, and soloed at sixteen, but failed to get an air force commission because he had twenty-thirty vision instead of the required twenty-twenty. For seventeen years, he was the chief jet pilot for the golf legend Arnold Palmer. His dream of flying fighter planes finally came true in 1987 when he and a partner won a contract to train navy test pilots to fly TF-51s and P-51s. Three years later, they founded Stallion 51.

A renowned instructor and air show ace, Lee now boasted over 6,000 hours flying Mustangs, more than any other pilot on record. On any given day, Stallion 51's hangars held a dozen or more vintage war birds, including Spitfires, T-6 Texans, P-51s, and TF-51s. The company provided services ranging from flying lessons to aircraft maintenance, restoration, and sales. There was even a full-time flight surgeon on staff.

Lee noted that only about 150 single-seat P-51 Mustangs remained from the more than 15,000 manufactured during World War II. They commanded prices of up to $2 million, and require annual operating expenses of roughly $100,000, including a whopping $30,000 for insurance. Not surprisingly, most current Mustang owners were wealthy doctors or investment bankers.

But thanks to Stallion 51, experiencing the thrill of flying a war bird was relatively cheap. A one-hour orientation flight in a two-seat TF-51 Mustang with Lee or one of his instructor pilots cost $2,950. A one-hour flight in a T-6 Texan, which required less maintenance and burned less fuel, was only $600.

Lee demonstrated some of the maneuvers we would perform in the TF-51 with model airplanes. They included an aileron roll, in which the plane turned over 360 degrees, and a barrel roll, in which the plane circumscribed a pattern similar to the inside rim of a barrel. I confessed that the mere thought of such aerobatics made my stomach churn.

"Your resistance to queasiness and g-forces is enhanced if you're flying the plane yourself," Lee assured.

My queasiness meter soared a few minutes later when Lee strapped me into the rear cockpit of Crazy Horse and pointed out the principal controls. The big black handle on my left was the throttle. The silvery trim wheel beside my seat adjusted the ailerons. The left and right foot pedals moved the rudder. The stick between my legs turned the plane and elevated or lowered the nose. The trigger on the stick, which once fired wing-mounted machine guns, engaged the intercom.

If we had to bail out, Lee said I should exit from the right side of the cockpit, and count to three to give myself time to fall clear of the wings before pulling the rip cord. I told him I'd never jumped out of an airplane.

"I haven't jumped either, and I don't want to ruin my record," Lee replied. "If we lose power, that doesn't necessarily mean I'll want to leave the airplane. I may be able to land it like a glider."

The next thing I knew, we were rolling, and I was alternately pressing the left and right rudder pedals. As Lee explained, the Mustang's nose was so high, we had to zigzag down the taxiway and peek out the sides to see where we were going. Enthralled by the rudder's responsiveness, I momentarily forgot my fears—only to realize I was veering the 9,200-pound plane perilously close to the edge of the pavement.

"I keep oversteering," I rasped into my boom mike.

"It's quite common," Lee returned. "But you're doing great, so no issues at all."

When we reached the end of runway 33, Lee reassumed control of the rudder pedals, and turned the

Mustang's blue conical nose into the wind. He revved the Merlin engine to 2,300 revolutions per minute and released the wheel brakes. We raced down the centerline until suddenly—miraculously, it seemed to me—we were airborne.

The earth fell away, and I saw white puffs of cumulus clouds billowing above the bubble canopy. Lee banked the Mustang sharply to the left. Then he leveled off, and advised that we were going about 180 miles an hour at an altitude of 1,400 feet.

"Harry, I'm going to put you back to work flying the airplane," he declared.

All I could think was, "God help us!"

A Novice Pilot Soars, and
His Doubts Fall

I hurtled toward the restricted military airspace over Avon Park Air Force Range in the rear cockpit of a TF-51 Mustang named "Crazy Horse," clutching the control stick between my legs. The World War II vintage instruments indicated the plane was going 300 miles per hour at an altitude of 7,500 feet some forty miles south of Kissimmee, Florida. It seemed, however, that I was in a slow-motion dream, sailing on a pale blue ocean frothing with cumulus cloud waves.

Save for witnessing my wife give birth to our son, flying the Mustang was by far the coolest, most humbling thing I'd ever done. It made me feel bolder than Batman, cockier than a barnyard rooster. At the same time, it also scared me silly.

I gave silent thanks that my fifty-five-year-old veteran instructor Lee Lauderback was in the forward cockpit ready to pounce on the Mustang's dual controls if I screwed up.

"Mustang Zero One," Lee rasped into his boom mike. "Range check?"

"We're cold at the moment, but we're waiting on a flight," the Avon Park controller advised. "Could be any time."

"Can we use it until you get hot again?" Lee pressed.

"Okay," the controller replied. "Just tell me where you're gonna be."

I stared out the Mustang's bubble canopy as Lee detailed our flight plan. We were passing over what appeared to be a pair of runways in the middle of nowhere. At the near end, there were some low-rise buildings, and a squadron of fighter jets. At the far end, there was a row of white patches that looked like gigantic sand boxes.

"That area that looks like an airport is a tactical firing range designed to resemble an Iraq or Afghanistan arrangement," Lee advised. "The buildings are supposed to be terrorist houses. The planes are actually plywood replicas of Soviet MiGs. The sandy areas with the rectangular lines are 20-millimeter strafing pits."

"They use live ammo out there?" I asked.

"Oh, yes, they do," Lee confirmed.

I felt my stomach do a double backflip. So far, I had performed only the most basic maneuvers in the Mustang: turning left, turning right, nosing up, nosing down. But under Lee's direction, I was supposed to attempt a series of aerobatics starting with an aileron roll that would literally make the plane do double backflips. "What this'll do is give you a lot more confidence about banked turns," Lee assured.

I sucked a deep breath, stalling for time. As Lee had demonstrated with a model airplane back on the ground, the ailerons were hinged control panels on the outboard ends of the wings that operated in tandem. When the right aileron went down, the left aileron went up, and vice versa, facilitating your ability to turn in either direction. In an aileron roll, you made the airplane flip over upside down and right side up again.

That sounded like an aerial circus trick, the kind of stunt hot dogs performed at air shows. But I knew both from background research and from long conversations with my late father, a former navy test pilot, that maneuvers like aileron rolls served deadly serious military purposes.

By virtually all accounts, the P-51 Mustang was the plane that enabled Allied forces to achieve air superiority over Germany in World War II. Following its combat debut in late 1943, the army's three main Mustang fighter groups claimed to have shot down 4,950 enemy aircraft, roughly 50 percent of all Allied "kills" in the European Theater. Those same three units also claimed to have destroyed another 4,131 aircraft on the ground, while losing only 840 of their own planes.

The secret to the Mustang's success was its unique combination of speed, range, and maneuverability. Thanks to a 1,700-horsepower Merlin engine designed by Rolls-Royce, it was fast enough to catch up with and destroy a V-1 rocket. No other propeller-driven plane could beat it in a straight-up vertical climb. Segueing from high-powered ascents into loops and rolls helped U.S. pilots avoid hostile fire and position themselves to attack enemy aircraft.

With less than ninety minutes of ground school training under my belt and only twenty minutes inside the cockpit of the Mustang, I had no illusions about having "the right stuff," much less becoming the next Chuck Yeager. In fact, a part of me wanted to beg Lee Lauderback to fly us right back to Kissimmee Gateway Airport. But much to my chagrin, there was another part of me that must have inherited my father's unadulterated love of flying, because I agreed to let Lee talk me through my first aileron roll.

"It's gonna feel a little weird to you," he allowed. "All your instincts are gonna tell you that you have to hold onto your seat, but you don't. You're gonna stay in your seat just like you are."

"Roger that," I replied with nary an ounce of conviction.

"The only important thing is just to keep holding the stick all the way over until I tell you to neutralize," Lee added. "Don't pull back. Don't push forward. Just keep it over there. We're gonna start by bringing up the nose."

I nodded, and tightened my grip on the control stick as the Mustang's propeller rose above the bowled horizon. My limbs and stomach clenched against the mounting g-force like they had just taken a volley of antiaircraft flak.

"Now turn it all the way to the left!" Lee cried out.

I shoved the stick toward my left knee and held it there as directed. Suddenly, earth and sky switched. I saw green and brown above, pale blue and puffy white below. Then, just as suddenly, earth and sky resumed their familiar places. I heard Lee tell me to neutralize the stick between my legs.

"Good job, good job," he cheered as the Mustang leveled off again.

Overcome with a wondrous mixture of relief, disbelief, and sheer joy, I shouted out a stream of triumphant expletives.

Moments later, I was doing a second aileron roll, this time flipping the plane over to the right. Then I did a barrel roll, elevating the nose and flopping over to trace the circumference of an imaginary barrel. For a split second, I felt the bliss of weightlessness. I celebrated with another burst of unprintable exclamations. Then I exited Avon Park Air Force Range before any live firing commenced.

"I think I'm gonna let you land it," Lee said.

That should have sobered me right up. Instead, I kept chortling like a drunken seaman as Lee talked me through our final approach to Kissimmee Gateway.

"Your first job is to line up with that centerline," he advised as the Mustang descended toward runway 33. "Now nose her up a little . . . Relax, you're doing fine . . . Pull back on the stick just a little bit more."

The wings teetered to the right. I nudged the stick

to the left, and they leveled. Then I heard the tires squeal against the tarmac as the Mustang made a perfect landing.

I tried to come to my senses as Lee taxied the plane back to the Stallion 51 hangars. I knew he had lowered the flaps and the landing gear. I suspected he had also worked considerable magic with the rudder pedals from takeoff to touchdown. But in the end, I didn't care. All I heard was the purr of the TF-51 Mustang named Crazy Horse, and words that were music to the earphones inside my blue Kevlar crash helmet.

"Maybe," Lee Lauderback said, "I'll make a fighter pilot out of you after all."

Man, Middle-Aged, Seeks Swimsuit

I crossed the shimmering sands of South Beach, blinking my eyes in the glare. It was a postcard-perfect pastel day on the perennially cool and hip lower tip of the barrier island that separates Miami from the infinite sea. I saw waves crashing. I heard umbrella poles creaking. I felt gull wings rustling my hair. Spring had sprung, and I was in executive pursuit of the perfect bathing suit.

OK, I know what you're thinking—some guys have all the luck. But it wasn't like that, I swear. My potentially prurient pursuit wasn't about ogling itsy-bitsy bikinis worn by impossibly beautiful women. Mine was a man's mission impossible. I was in search of a bathing suit that a somewhat less than perfectly fit middle-aged dude like me could actually wear in public.

Attired in a golf shirt and khaki trousers, I began to grasp the true enormity of my challenge as I trudged toward the ocean. At first, the entire strand seemed to be teeming with perfectly proportioned aliens from a fat-free planet. Along with fastidiously figured females in itsy-bitsy bikinis, I encountered males in thigh-length and knee-length swimsuits with the chiseled physiques of Greek statues.

Then I spied what appeared to be a beached whale in briefs. He was lying on a towel near the lapping surf in a semifetal position, legs tucked, eyes closed, arms wrapped around his shaved head. His posterior and private parts were bound up, but just barely, in a black nylon Speedo that exposed a bulbous, sun-burned belly and tanning lotion-slathered thighs. I stared at him for a full minute, aghast and perversely elated. Then I turned and fled for the art deco district.

I tried to dispel the haunting images of my star-crossed trek to the strand by focusing on swimwear financials. Bathing attire generates over $12 billion in annual worldwide sales, according to Dow Fiber Solutions, a unit of the Dow Chemical Company. Reliable statistics on men's sales are harder to come by than a nightclub VIP room pass. But my instincts and the preponderance of anecdotal evidence suggested they were (pun intended) relatively modest compared with women's sales.

Instincts and anecdotes were confirmed when I entered the Ritchie's store at 160 8th Street. Born as a one-man shop in 1981, the privately held firm now had four locations in south Florida, and celebrity clients like Molly Sims, Pamela Anderson, and Toni Braxton. I discovered the eponymous founder Ritchie Berger had decided not to produce a men's line for 2006. "The women's line just sells better," a female clerk noted.

Indeed, the evolution of modern swimwear has revolved around women since the French invented the bikini in 1946. The Australian sportswear-maker Speedo caused the first postwar revolution in men's fashion by introducing briefs for competitors at the 1956 Olympics in Melbourne. According to Speedo, athletes wearing its products went on to win 70 percent of all swimming medals in the 1968, 1972, and 1976 Olympics. Such feats transformed the brand into an icon synonymous with briefs, even though other companies also manufactured them.

The late 1960s inspired a fashion antithesis as surfers began wearing cut-offs, which were typically denim jeans with the legs clipped above the knee. Soon iconoclastic designers like Quiksilver, another Australian firm founded in 1969, were offering far more colorful "board shorts" made of fast-drying polyester fabrics that dropped down to, and eventually below, the knee. In 2005, Quiksilver reported $1.6 billion in sales from swimwear and assorted sportswear.

Speedo, meanwhile, had gone from minimal to maximum skin coverage. It had recently introduced full-body athletic suits made of fabric that purportedly replicated the aquadynamics of sharkskin and cost over $400. Now a unit of the Warnaco Group known as Authentic Fitness Corporation, the company said only 2 percent of its $65 million in sales came from swim briefs, which I figured was probably a good thing for all concerned.

But after my encounters on the strand, I approached the local Quiksilver store at 750 Collins Avenue with trepidation. I had always sympathized if never quite identified with women like my wife who felt pressured to diet down to semianorexia before donning any swimsuit. Was there still a double standard? Was it propagated, perpetuated, and reinforced by mass media fashionistas and *Sports Illustrated*'s annual swimsuit issue? Well, duh!

I realized, however, there was also a kind of a triple

standard I shared with most of my male buddies. It used to be that guys like me could flaunt sub-Adonis physiques on the beach without fear or shame. In the wake of the fitness craze, those days were as done as disco. Few things were more appalling to men than the sight of another male in a bathing suit he wasn't cut out to wear. I shuddered at the thought of what I'd look like in a swimsuit after a long dark calorie-consuming winter.

I found out shortly after I slipped past the two red surfboards guarding the entrance to the Quiksilver store. I was greeted by Luelle Llorens, age nineteen, and Jen Courtney, age twenty-two. Louella ushered me directly to a dressing room, while Jen fetched an assortment of men's designer swimwear.

The man who presently appeared in the dressing room mirror bore a frightening resemblance to the beached whale in briefs, but he had ghoulishly white skin and a Quiksilver logo on his black nylon-covered bottom. I cracked open the door, warning that these $16 briefs were far too brief for me. "They show everything and, wow, I don't really want to see that," Jen agreed.

I shut the door, and tried on a pair of $49.50 harlequin-patterned boxer trunks from the store's Retro Collection. Where the briefs measured just twelve inches from waist to crotch bottom, the trunks spanned sixteen inches, but they were only marginally more becoming on my love-handled torso.

Luella tossed over a $45 charcoal-patterned swimsuit from the Silver Edition. It measured nineteen inches long and featured a flab-forgiving elastic waistband. "This style is popular with older surfers who aren't that fit," she noted.

Wincing, I asked what young fit surfers wore. Jen offered some $52 board shorts glowing with red, white, blue, pink, and black juxtaposed patterns. They hung a full twenty-two inches, covering my knees, and they came with a surfing DVD titled *Wild Guns II*. The board shorts were my customary size 36, but their nonelastic waistband pinched my love handles as badly as the trunks.

Jen suggested I try a size 38 or a size 40. I insisted on the 38s, only to find to my shock and chagrin that they slipped way down below my belly button to the upper perimeter of my privates.

"Actually, they're supposed to fit that way," Luella noted.

"Those are like, 'Bah!'" Jen observed. "How could you not notice them?"

I bought the board shorts, the old fogey Silver Edition swimsuit, and a hooded sweatshirt for my long-suffering wife. Then I departed Quiksilver to sample one last, even more risqué option—the thong.

I found it at Deco Denim at 645 Collins Avenue. Blue with tropical splashes of red and yellow, it measured just six inches from waist to crotch bottom. But its low-slung elastic banding secured my privates without pinching my love handles. And the price was only $12.99. Unfortunately, the thong exposed far more than the briefs. It gave me a nauseous, spine-tingling chill.

Vowing to live at the gym and never eat solid food again, I ventured back onto the strand. It was just before sunset, waves retreating, umbrellas folding, gulls feasting on litter. The beached whale in briefs was gone. A squadron of perfectly proportioned local firemen in red trunks had taken his place, and they were flirting with some impossibly beautiful women in itsy-bitsy bikinis.

None of them said "Bah!"—or even seemed to notice—as I peeled off my golf shirt and rolled my khaki trousers above my knees.

A Boy of Summer Who
Prefers Melee

I sensed that a serious ball was in play when I saw my eight-year-old son, Harrison, run out of the house clutching a glass of water. It was a luscious spring afternoon on eastern Long Island with scarcely a cloud in the sky and the backyard blooming like a field of suburban dreams. But Harrison was grimacing as if he was in the throes of an apocalyptic nightmare.

"Dad! Dad!" he cried, scrambling across the driveway to my office shack. "Do you know how to make water vapor?"

"Is this an experiment for science class?" I asked. Harrison flashed a grin that made the braces on his front teeth sparkle like mischievous silverfish. "I want to make water vapor so it'll rain tomorrow," he said. "Then I won't have to go to Little League baseball practice."

I snatched the glass from Harrison's hand. "What would you rather do?"

"Stay home and play video games," he replied, batting both eyes.

I was simultaneously dismayed and overcome by a confounded parent's unconditional love of child. Right then and there I made a silent oath to embark on a special executive pursuit in honor of Father's Day.

Instead of pursuing ever faster, fancier forms of hedonism, I would chase an even more elusive goal. I would strive to gain a better, deeper understanding of my ostensibly nonathletic son by doing the parental two-step. First, I'd take a fresh look at Little League baseball. Then, I'd sample the video games he wanted to play.

I realized I was already caught in a merciless metaphorical rundown between a third-grader and the home plate umpire. My wife, Alison, had insisted on enrolling Harrison in the Sag Harbor Little League program that season and the previous one for all the right-minded reasons. Alison believed it would build his confidence, teach him teamwork and tenacity, and save two hours worth of babysitting fees three times a week. What working parent could fault her for that?

And yet, I secretly shared Harrison's distaste for competitive sports in general and Little League in particular. Inept at baseball, I had played competitive golf from age ten to nineteen. But I played golf on my own volition because I was blessed and cursed with a genuine love of the game. Along the way, I learned that few monsters were more destructive than wrong-minded macho stage parents who forced their children to pursue their frustrated sports fantasies. I owed it to Harrison and to myself not to become one of them.

The next day dawned ominously sunny and bright, and baseball practice became as inevitable as misguided parental expectations. Before Harrison's school let out, I did my due diligence on the evolution of Little League baseball. Founded in 1939 with three teams in Williamsport, Pennsylvania, it was the first—and for many years the only—organized sport widely accessible to children five to eighteen.

At its peak in 1996, Little League was in all 50 states and 105 countries, and had annual participation of just under 3 million players, according to a league spokesman, Chris Downs. Much of the boom was fueled by Asia and Latin America. From 1967 to

2003, twenty-eight of the thirty-six World Series winning teams came from outside the United States, specifically Japan, Taiwan, South Korea, and Venezuela.

But by 2005, Little League's reach had shrunk to 70 countries and roughly 2.5 million players. Mr. Downs said one reason was that Little League was no longer the only kid on the block. Organized youth sports in the United States had grown far beyond traditional games like baseball, basketball, and football to include everything from soccer and skateboarding to rollerblading and BMX racing.

To my chagrin, Mr. Downs also said that the booming video game industry, which had annual sales of over $9 billion in the United States according to the NPD Group, a market research firm based in Port Washington, New York, had contributed to Little League's decline in popularity. "The children of today are much more computer savvy than any of their parents were growing up," he noted. "It almost parallels the early years of Little League when most families didn't have television sets. Then television sets came into the home, and kids started spending more and more time playing indoors."

I felt marginally reassured to know that my son was part of a historic global trend rather than a lonely odd kid out. But my attitude toward our local

Little League soured when Harrison and I arrived at the ballpark at the designated five P.M. starting time.

Having taught golf to seven- and eight-year-olds, I appreciated mentoring challenges and admired people who volunteered to take them on. But the coaches seemed to reverse roles with the children. The game didn't get under way until quarter to six. It was supposed to last only five innings, with a five-run limit on per-inning scoring by each team. Instead, it went six full innings because the coaches insisted on breaking the 13–13 tie that resulted at the end of five.

As it turned out, Harrison got two hits on the day, and his team won the game. But by that time, most of my fellow parents and I wanted to boil the coaches into water vapor. It was quarter to eight. Our children had been on the field for almost three hours. They hadn't eaten dinner, bathed, or done their homework, and they all had to go to school in the morning.

"I hate baseball!" Harrison hollered when we got home at last. Then he slumped face-first on his chicken nuggets.

The following afternoon, I played Harrison's favorite video game, *Super Smash Brothers Melee,* which, of course, came from Japan. The way his eyes lit up when we sat down at the consoles signaled that another edifying role reversal was at hand. "It's about how you die, Dad," he explained. "The person who dies the most loses."

We began by choosing our respective characters. Harrison picked Dr. Mario, and I settled on Pikachu. The next thing I knew, a battle commenced in a futuristic city teeming with flying machines. Dr. Mario and Pikachu traded punches in a blaze of audiovisual pyrotechnics that overloaded my senses and left me panting for breath.

I marveled at Harrison's video game mastery. While *Super Smash Brothers Melee* didn't demand the running, throwing, and hitting skills of baseball, it required manual dexterity, timing, and strategy far beyond my parental capabilities. I winced in frustration as Harrison defeated me by a score roughly equivalent to 250 to zip.

"It's just a game. It's supposed to be fun," he reminded me. "You're having fun, aren't you, Dad?"

I nodded and steeled myself for a second battle that took place in a weird mushroom kingdom. Harrison won by another lopsided score. The venue switched to a castle, and we switched characters. Harrison won yet again. But when we got to Pokemon Stadium, I somehow managed to eke out a victory in sudden death.

"Yahoo!" I hollered triumphantly. "That's more like it!"

"Way to go, Dad!" Harrison cheered.

Then, as if to let me know he'd been toying with me all along, Harrison beat me five more times in less than fifteen minutes. I conceded defeat on all levels.

"We have to finish this season of Little League so Mom doesn't get mad at us," I allowed. "But if you still hate baseball when it's over, we'll pour gasoline on your bat and glove and set them on fire. They'll burn into smoke and water vapor."

Harrison frowned at his video game console, pondering my proposal. Finally, he looked up, and flashed a silverfish grin.

"Dad, I have a better idea," he declared. "Why don't we paint them white and hang them on the wall so we can't see them, and we can forget about the whole thing."

Agape with wonder at the way my son had just hit the ball out of the park, I said that would be the best Father's Day present ever.

Act Five

READY FOR SOME FOOTBALL? THEN HOW ABOUT BALLET?

A Paper Jet Recalls Plimpton, If Not Namath

I ripped off my werewolf mask and raced down the Southern State Parkway under a Halloween moon shaped like a giant orange football. Shortly before midnight, I checked into a fourth-floor room at the Long Island Marriott in Hempstead, New York. At 6:45 the following morning, I drove across the street to the New York Jets training facility on the campus of Hofstra University to report for a tryout at quarterback.

I reckoned it wouldn't do to come into the National Football League quoting Camus or Dostoevsky, so I approached the parking lot security gate with a Stevie Ray Vaughan CD cranked to full volume. "You can't change it, can't rearrange it," Stevie Ray hollered. "Time is all that we got, so baby, let's take it."

At 7:04 A.M., I entered the equipment room, where they measured my head for a helmet. They probably should have put me in a straight jacket. My particular madness was inspired by my late friend George Plimpton. In 1965, he published *Paper Lion,* which recounted his adventures as a writer turned "last-string quarterback" for the Detroit Lions who ran five epic, tragicomic plays in an intrasquad scrimmage during their preseason training camp.

Over the summer, I'd heard that the New York Jets owner Woody Johnson was an avid Plimpton fan, and I persuaded him to let me try a similar pursuit as an homage to George. Woody agreed that I could run three plays at quarterback in an intrasquad scrimmage during the midseason bye week when the team did not have a Sunday game. I would get the chance to live out every couch potato's ultimate football fantasy by becoming a "Paper Jet."

As I plopped down on a stool in the equipment room, my fifty-four-year-old body suddenly felt more like a piece of papier-mâché with severe stomach cramps. The equipment manager Gus Granneman picked up on my condition or lack thereof when I tried unsuccessfully to squeeze my head into one of his spare helmets. "It's been awhile, huh?" he grunted.

My face flushed with embarrassment and primal fear. The last time I'd put on a football uniform was four decades ago. I was a fourteen-year-old tight end who was far more interested in catching passes than blocking linebackers. The next year, my parents insisted I quit tackle football to concentrate on golf. My quarterbacking experience was limited to a score of touch football games contested mostly in backyards and on beaches.

Gus helped me into the helmet, and pumped air through a hole in the top, inflating the pads inside until my head felt like it was going to burst. I tried on some white uniform pants with green stripes down the legs and a set of shoulder pads. The pants felt snugger than ballet tights, and the shoulder pads pinched my ears as they came on and off.

Gus's staff set me up at a movable dressing cubicle in the player's lounge next to the main locker room. I took off my street clothes and slipped into a green fleece jumpsuit. Then I headed up to the second floor for the eight A.M. quarterbacks meeting in offensive coordinator Brian Schottenheimer's office with starter Chad Pennington and backups Patrick Ramsey and Kellen Clemens.

One of the most startling things about being around pro football players in person as opposed to watching them on TV is realizing how extraterrestrially big they are, even the "little guys" who play quarterback. Listed in the program at six feet three and 225 pounds, Chad was an inch taller but two dozen pounds heavier than me, none of it flab. His neck was nearly as thick as one of my thighs, his wrists were easily the size of my forearms, and his fingers looked strong enough to squeeze a pigskin until it oinked.

Brian clicked on a video screen and we watched film clips of the Jets' first eight games. A front office staffer popped in and asked me to sign a waiver. Along with releasing the Jets from any and all liability, it noted that my participation in the scrimmage scheduled for that afternoon involved "risk of physical injury and death."

I flipped through a black spiral notebook labeled "New York Jets Offensive Game Plan Book." Chad's notebook contained diagrams of well over a hundred plays. Mine contained three plays. The first was named "Jack Right Close 20 Mike," and I recognized it as a simple draw play. It called for me to pretend I was going to throw a pass, and then hand the ball off to the tailback.

I recognized the other two plays as passes, but I

was stumped by their long, obtuse names, "Double Right Gone Right 444 H Swing Flat" and "Flank Right Quick Ace Right 321 F Flat." I asked Brian if they were rollouts.

"No, no, we're not gonna roll you out today," he replied. "One play's a five-step drop, the other's a three-step drop."

"Quarterbacks on this team are born to walk, not run," Chad interjected.

Patrick and Kellen laughed, so I did.

Brian explained that the play calls consisted of four parts. The first two words designated the formation. The next few words specified the linemen's blocking assignments. The numbers indicated what routes the receivers should run. "H Swing Flat" and "F Flat" gave the halfback and the fullback their respective routes.

I spent the rest of the morning rehearsing my three plays at a conference table with the offensive quality control coach Jason Michael. He taught me how to hand the ball off on the running play, and the progression of receivers I should look for on the passing plays from primary to secondary to tertiary.

Jason also advised me on huddle etiquette. He told me to enter the huddle from the left side, then call the play and the snap cadence twice. But instead of saying "on two" like schoolboy quarterbacks, I was supposed to say, "Second sound, second sound." After I crouched behind the center at the line of scrimmage, I'd simply shout the first sound, "Set!" and then the second sound, "Hut!"

"You've got to take control in the huddle," Jason said, "just like Chad does."

At 11:45 A.M., I went back down to the players lounge to suit up. I found a red jersey in my dressing cubicle. In an effort to limit injuries to valuable quarterbacks during practices, NFL coaches typically give them red jerseys, warning that they are not to be tackled by defensive players. My red jersey was numbered "0," the same number Plimpton wore for the Detroit Lions.

Laveranues Coles, the Jets' star wide receiver, wandered into the lounge wearing football pants and a green knit cap. When I told him I was planning to throw him a pass, his pointy eyes widened in disbelief. "You're gonna get yourself killed out there," he said.

I ventured into the main locker room, hoping to make friends with some offensive linemen. I was quickly accosted by Justin Miller, a five-feet-ten, 196-pound cornerback and kickoff returner. Justin said he was going to cripple me with an all-out blitz. I forced a smile, and tugged on my red jersey.

"I'm color-blind," Justin declared, glowering at me.

Pete Kendall, the veteran offensive guard, roared with laughter. At six feet five and 292 pounds, Pete was terrific at blocking blitzing cornerbacks. He was also regarded as one of the Jets' most intelligent and quotable players. As it turned out, he had read Plimpton's book, and he understood what I was trying to accomplish.

"I bet this idea looked a whole lot better on paper than it does right now," he allowed.

Moments later, I watched Pete, Justin, Laveranues, Chad, and the rest of the team trot out to the practice field, leaving me alone in the locker room to contemplate my impending fate amid the smells of liniment and freshly washed jocks.

A Paper Jet Seizes the Moment with a Quick Ace Right

I caught my reflection in the doors of the New York Jets locker room and almost dropped my helmet. I figured it was a judgment call as to whether I looked scarier in my football uniform with the red number "0" jersey or in the werewolf costume with the gray fake fur I'd worn the night before on Halloween.

Before I could seek an official ruling, the digital clock on the locker room wall flashed 2:15. It was time for me to take the field as a writer in executive pursuit of becoming an NFL quarterback. I had three plays to run. They would show whether I was a "Paper Jet" worthy of carrying on the tradition my late friend George Plimpton established with his 1965 bestseller *Paper Lion,* or just another dreamer without a throwing arm.

I pulled on my helmet and burst through the locker room doors.

The afternoon sun was piercing a daylong cloud cover. I could see virtually the entire Jets roster working out on the practice field. Save for the other quarterbacks who had red jerseys like mine signifying we were off-limits to tacklers, half of the players wore white jerseys with green numbers and the other half wore green with white numbers. Concert-volume rap music blared from outdoor speakers.

The offensive coordinator Brian Schottenheimer waved me to the sidelines for a final dress rehearsal. Nick Mangold, a six-four, 300-pound rookie center, crouched over to deliver my first practice snaps. I was mortally afraid Nick would hike the ball so hard my hands would break. But he laid it in my palms like a pigskin pillow.

My second fear was that I'd suffer a fifty-four-year-old's senior moment and forget how to call my three plays. I actually blurted the correct words, but my voice was so loud it could be heard out on the adjacent turnpike. "Keep your voice down in the huddle," the starting quarterback Chad Pennington admonished, "like you're having a conversation."

As I turned away to throw a few warm-up passes, I spotted the team owner, Woody Johnson, standing nearby in a blazer, tie, and green Jets cap. I glimpsed the head coach Eric Mangini hunkering on the far sideline in a black jumpsuit. Then the rap music stopped. I heard Brian calling my name, and I bolted out onto the field.

The instant I joined the gaggle of white jerseys in the huddle, I felt like I was going to throw up. I didn't recognize the other players on either side of the ball. There was no Justin Miller to blitz me, but there was no Pete Kendall to block, no Laveranues Coles to catch. The center wasn't Nick Mangold, but a No. 71 whom I'd never met, much less taken snaps from.

"You gotta take control," I whispered to myself, "just like Chad."

I put my hands on my knees and sucked a deep breath. All I could see was dirt and the battered shins of ten enormous men. All I could hear was Brian's voice crackling in my headset, reminding me to call the draw play I'd learned that morning.

"Jack Right Close 20 Mike," I said, stuttering. "Second sound, second sound."

My offensive unit broke out of the huddle, and I followed No. 71 up to the line of scrimmage. The defensive unit was already heckling me.

"Come on, number zero," one of them shouted. "Let's get it on."

"This is bye week," growled another. "We're ready for vacation."

I put my hands under No. 71's butt. His jersey was soaked, and perspiration was raining down on his pants.

"Set!" I shouted at the top of my lungs. "Hut!"

To my amazement, I took the snap without fumbling or tripping. I backpedaled a few steps, and stuck the ball into the onrushing gut of the tailback, who turned out to be Leon Washington, a five-eight, 202-pound rookie. I kept rolling out to my right, "finishing" the play without the ball like I'd seen Chad do on television. Then I glanced back, and saw Leon plunge forward for a five-yard gain.

I felt a joyous adrenaline rush. With that one successful handoff I'd bested Plimpton, who had fumbled repeatedly and lost a total of twenty-nine yards on the five plays he ran with the Detroit Lions. But Leon returned to the huddle rubbing his belly in pain.

"You don't have to jam it in there so hard, man," he complained.

I nodded, muttering an apology. Then I called my first pass play, trying to keep my overexcited voice at the conversational level Chad had recommended.

"Double Right Gone Right 444 H Swing Flat," I hissed.

I took the snap okay and dropped back five steps. My primary receiver was a tight end buttonhooking over the middle. But the linemen in front of me were so tall, I lost sight of him. I heaved the ball downfield as hard as I could. It barely missed the helmet of one of the opposing linebackers, and fell harmlessly to the turf.

"Get 'em in the huddle," Coach Mangini shouted from behind me.

I sensed that the other players were growing increasingly impatient, but this third play was likely to be the final one of my NFL career. As I reentered the huddle, I silently vowed to stay in the moment as long as it lasted.

"Flank Right Quick Ace Right 321 F Flat," I wheezed.

The huddle broke before I could call the snap cadence, but I figured just about everyone in Nassau County knew it was going to be on the second sound. As I sidled up to the center, I heard Brian's voice crackling in my headset.

"Corner's laying off," he said. "Go to the Big Alert."

Translated from the Jets playbook jargon, that

was the next thing to an audible. My primary receiver on the play was the fullback drifting out in the flat on the right side. But if the opposing cornerback to my left positioned himself more than a few yards back of the line of scrimmage, I was supposed to go to my left-side wideout, a.k.a. the Big Alert.

A split second later, I took the snap, whirled to my left, and chucked the ball toward a receiver who turned out to be Justin McCareins, a six-two, 215-pound speedster. The ball seemed to waffle in the air like a wounded duck. But somehow Justin made the grab. He raced upfield for a putative first down. I ran after him, waving a finger in the air like I was Joe Willie Namath winning Super Bowl III.

The four minutes that followed were an unforgettable blur. Leon leaped up and gave me a congratulatory chest butt that almost knocked me to the ground. One of the coaches called for me to "break it down" with my offensive unit by leading a cheer. We gathered in a circle, and stacked hands. But I had no idea what to do next. After a couple of false starts, I finally managed, "1-2-3 Go Jets!"

Brian beckoned me to break it down with Chad and his backups, Patrick Ramsey and Kellen Clemens, as if they were accepting me as one of their own. At Chad's suggestion, I hollered, "1-2-3 QBs!"

After we split, I overheard him say, "One for two's not bad. I'm proud of him. He handled it well."

Coach Mangini sauntered over. I was so elated, I asked if he'd sign me to a contract. He smiled sympathetically, then poured a bit of bitter over all the sweet. "It doesn't look good," he said.

I pumped his hand anyway, and said I'd talk to Woody.

I finally came back to earth forty-eight hours later when I watched a DVD of my performance with my nine-year-old son, Harrison. A soccer player destined to become a Nobel Prize–winning artist, entrepreneur, and brain surgeon, Harrison insisted that trick-or-treating as father and son werewolves on Halloween was much scarier than quarterbacking the Jets in an intrasquad scrimmage.

"It wasn't a real game, Dad," he noted. "But if you ever do get to play in a real game, you should wear that red jersey."

The Man Who Traded His Jets Uniform for Woolen Leg Warmers

I took my first tentative steps in executive pursuit of ballet when I tiptoed up to the door of an apartment building in Lower Manhattan. It was one of the coldest days of the year. My fifty-five-year-old muscles and bones were wrapped in layers of cotton, cashmere, and wool. But I felt like I was going to freeze into an ice sculpture before I even managed to learn the difference between a plié and a pirouette.

Charles Askegaard answered my buzz. He was wearing tan corduroys and a red turtleneck, and he stood six feet four with legs that seemed to stretch all the way to his hometown of Minneapolis. With a touch more avoirdupois on his fat-free 185-pound frame, he would've had the ideal physique to play wide receiver for the New York Jets. In fact, he was a thirty-eight-year-old principal dancer at the New York City Ballet.

"Have you got my shoes?" I blurted without even bothering to say hello.

"Yep," he replied. "But I still need to stitch the ankle straps."

Charles invited me inside his apartment for a high-protein breakfast of egg whites and unbuttered wheat toast. Once again, I tiptoed. It was eight A.M., and his wife, the author Candace Bushnell of *Sex and the City* fame, was still fast asleep.

As Charles whipped up the egg whites, I poured out my soul. For the last two weeks, I'd suffered merciless teasing whenever I said that I was going to try ballet dancing. Many of my tormenters were ignorant homophobes who made crude jokes about me being a "sissie." But the most galling remarks had come from some highly accomplished people I thought ought to know better.

The former editor of a major newsweekly asked if I was going to wear tights or a tutu. A female author of bestselling nonfiction books asked if I was going to shave my legs. A famous male novelist, who happened to be an old pal of Candace's, wished me luck, and then declared with a rueful grin, "Charles is always having to explain himself."

Charles dished out the egg whites, nodding sympathetically. He said he'd gotten unmitigated grief from his schoolmates, especially the other boys, after he started taking ballet lessons at age five. "In the eighth and ninth grades, I beat up about six of those guys," he recalled. "The teasing stopped after that."

As we rode the subway to Lincoln Center, I silently reviewed my historical due diligence. Ballet made its debut during the Italian Renaissance as a dinnertime divertissement for the court. In the mid-seventeenth century, Louis XIV, who was called the "Sun King" after one of his own ballet costumes, standardized and codified the art with the French terms still used in classical ballet today.

When Charles ushered me through the stage door of the New York State Theater, I realized I was entering a shrine of American dance. The New York City Ballet was cofounded in 1948 by George Balanchine, a Russian émigré who became the most acclaimed choreographer of the twentieth century. Balanchine's protégés included Jerome Robbins, who also choreographed Broadway hits like *West Side Story,* and Peter Martins, a Danish-born former dancer who has reigned as ballet master in chief since 1990.

The New York Times ballet critic Anna Kisselgoff once noted that Balanchine took forty years to educate his public "to appreciate dance for dance's sake." With Charles's insider guidance, I was hoping to educate myself in a single day by participating in the ballet's regular morning workout class and then trying to perform a fifteen-second routine.

My increasingly embarrassing moments of truth began when Charles and I entered his second-floor dressing room to change into ballet clothes. First, I donned a ballet belt, which was basically a heavily padded jock with a thick elastic waistband. Then I pulled on black nylon tights, white woolen leg warmers, a pink golf shirt, and a hooded sweat suit with a Texas Longhorn logo.

Unlike most athletic shoes, my white leather ballet shoes did not come ready to wear out of the box. Charles had to sew on the ankle straps with a needle and thread, and trim the drawstrings with scissors. "Most dancers sew their own shoes," he told me. "A lot of them are very superstitious about it."

A few minutes later, we entered a fifth-floor practice room with a padded gray Marley floor and mirrored walls lined with ballet barres. As I stripped off my sweats, I stole a glance at my reflection. It was not a pretty sight. The man in the mirror needed to lose fifteen pounds around his middle and tone all four limbs. I tried to take solace in a famous Balanchine dictum: "The mirror is not you—the mirror is you looking at yourself."

Charles tutored me in the five foot positions and a few moves that provided the building blocks of ballet. The tights made my legs feel surprisingly springy, but trying to assume the correct positions proved to be pretty excruciating. First position, for example, called for me to stand with heels touching and toes splayed out at a 180-degree angle. Fifth position required a similar splay, with the heel of my front foot against the toes of my back foot.

"You just need a little more turnout from the hips," Charles advised as I tottered and tripped over my own feet.

The move that came easiest for me was the tendu. All I had to do was grip the ballet barre with one hand and point the toes of my opposite-side foot forward, backward, and outward. The killer moves were the pliés from first position and fifth position. The demi-plié called for a relatively slight bending of the knees in a half squat. But I felt a sharp twinge in my lower back every time I came back up. The grand plié required an even deeper knee bend that made my cartilage burn like bacon grease.

My physical and emotional discomfort shifted into high gear when Charles led me into the main hall for the regular 10:30 A.M. workout class. The room was filled with more than fifty dancers, over half of the entire company, casually attired in leotards, tights, and sweats. I stood next to Charles in his usual spot beside a bevy of ballerinas who were less than half my age. Then I clutched the ballet barre with a trembling hand.

Moments later, Sean Lavery, the assistant to the ballet master, called the opening combinations. The piano player played some classical music, and the room became a blur of bodies performing pliés and tendus. Though seldom on balance and never in step, I managed to hang in for a little over half an hour. Georgina Pazcoguin, a sprightly brunette who had danced in the corps de ballet for over four years, offered encouragement even as she giggled at my ineptitude.

"Just try to go with the flow," she whispered.

Suddenly, the piano player struck up a fast-paced medley of Broadway show tunes. The other dancers began bounding across the room like two-legged gazelles. I quickly retreated to a corner for my safety and theirs, watching in awe. I knew the artistic styles of their leaps descended from the likes of Nijinsky,

Nureyev, and Baryshnikov. But their athleticism—and their air time—matched that of a Michael Jordan making a slam dunk from the top of the circle.

After class, Charles and I changed back into street clothes and went out for coffee. Every joint in my body already ached, and all we had done was warm up. That afternoon I was supposed to pair with Jenifer Ringer, a ballerina with whom Charles was going to perform on stage that night. My spine shivered in trepidation when he said that she would expect me to provide support through every step of our pas de deux.

"The male dancer is like a human ballet barre," Charles informed me. "You've got to be the rock."

Paper Balanchine

Charles Askegaard and I crossed Lincoln Center plaza bundled in navy overcoats with tote bags slung over our shoulders like a couple of accountants on a lunch-hour exercise break. It was a frigid mid-February afternoon. The winter wind cut through to my already aching middle-aged bones. Even my ultra-fit thirty-eight-year-old buddy, a principal dancer at the New York City Ballet, felt the pain.

"This is bad weather for ballet dancers," Charles said as we circumnavigated the fountains. "Back when we had the warm spell around Christmas, things were great. But since it's turned cold, I've gotten tendonitis in my Achilles tendons."

"I must have tendonitis in my prefrontal lobes," I replied, shivering.

I reckoned only a form of brain damage could have inspired me to embark on the preposterous executive pursuit of trying to learn ballet dancing. And now it was getting serious. Having spent the morning learning some basics, I was going to attempt a specially choreographed fifteen-second routine with the prima ballerina who was scheduled to dance on stage that night with Charles.

Charles and I ducked into a dressing room on the eighth floor of the Rose Building to change into our ballet clothes. I remembered that George Balanchine, the legendary Russian émigré choreographer who co-founded the New York City Ballet, had a passionate pas de deux policy: "In my ballets, woman is first. Men are consorts. God made men to sing the praises of women. They are not equal to men. They are better."

To my chagrin, Charles offered a slightly more male-oriented perspective based on his own dancing experience. "Ballet is like ballroom dancing: Someone has to take the lead," he told me. "When you're partnering, the man is really in the driver's seat. You need to be strong. You have to assert yourself in a very distinct way to give her the support she needs. But you also have to let her shine. I like to give my partners some freedom, so something unexpected can happen."

As if on cue, something unexpected happened within seconds. On our way down a staircase, I saw my dancing partner for the first time. Her name was Jenifer Ringer, and she was curled up on a couch in an alcove off one of the landings with a white down jacket pulled over her like a blanket. As we passed, she blinked open her eyes, groaning.

"Rehearsal's at 2:30, right?" she asked.

"Yep," Charles replied. "You're fine. Go back to sleep."

My watch showed 2:02 P.M. civilian time but, as Charles noted, it was almost midnight company time. The New York City Ballet's winter season ran from November 21, 2006, to February 25, 2007. During that period, the dancers worked out and rehearsed six days a week in precisely timed intervals. The principals performed on stage no less than three days a week, and twice a day on matinee weekends—all this for top salaries in the $80,000 to $120,000 range.

"Everybody's burned out this time of year," Charles confided. "You have to grab a nap whenever you can."

We entered a seventh-floor rehearsal room with a padded gray Marley floor and mirrored walls lined with ballet barres. Charles told me that Jenifer and I would be performing a segment from act two of *Swan Lake*. He obligingly refreshed my memory of the storyline.

I was Prince Siegfried, and Jenifer was Odette, a beautiful girl who changed into a white swan every night under the spell of the evil magician Von Rothbart. The only way Odette could be freed from the spell was if I swore my love for her. But Von Rothbart was going to trick me into swearing my love for a black swan named Odile, whose part was typically danced by the same ballerina who danced the part of Odette.

I thanked the ballet gods that Charles and I were alone as we blocked my moves. It had been embarrassing enough to participate in the company's morning workout class wearing a golf shirt with my black tights. Now I was wearing a baby-blue form-fitting performance top Charles had picked out at Capezio. My reflection in the mirror looked more like a blue-bellied whale than a handsome prince in love with a swan.

My anxiety level soared to balletic heights when Jenifer entered the room in a black leotard, and plopped down on the floor to put on her toe shoes. Raised in South Carolina, she had danced with the New York City Ballet for over sixteen years, touring the world with Charles and the other members of the company. She had a rosebud mouth, brunette ringlets, and bruised feet bulging with bunions. The first thing she did was wrap her toes with tape. "It's because of the friction," she explained. "Sometimes you get blisters."

"Charles says I'm in love with you, and I'm filled with longing," I informed her.

"And I'm a little scared of you," Jenifer replied in character.

I didn't blame her. Our routine was fraught with potential pitfalls. She was to begin lying on the floor bent forward from the waist like a sleeping swan. I was to walk over, take her by the wrists with my thumbs and middle fingers, and raise her onto the tips of her toe shoes so that she was balanced en pointe. She would lower her left arm, and pirouette to the right. I would grasp her waist as she tilted forward and to the left in an arabesque penché.

Then Jenifer would walk away three steps to the right. I would catch up, grasp her waist, guide her through another arabesque tilting forward and to the right, and promenade her around in a circle. She would walk away three steps to the left. I would grasp her by the waist once again, and lift her off the floor in a loving climax.

But as I discovered in our prerehearsals, simply walking across the floor in time with a tape recording of Tchaikovsky's score was problematic. I was accustomed to walking heel-toe. Ballet dancers walk toe-heel, which is roughly like trying to tiptoe on eggshells. I could hear myself gasping and wheezing with every step.

Jenifer's lithe leg strength made it relatively easy for me to raise her en pointe. Keeping her there was another matter. Time and again, I tipped her off balance by pulling her too far back toward me.

"I'm afraid that I'm going to push you down on your nose," I apologized.

"You won't," Jenifer assured me. "But if you do, that's okay. Then I won't have to dance tonight."

My attempts at executing the lift were even more laughable. As Charles explained, the trick was to gain the power and momentum to raise Jenifer up by first doing a plié, the ballet equivalent of a deep knee bend. Jenifer barely weighed a hundred pounds. But in the wake of the morning workout class, my knees were about as flexible as a two-by-four, and my arms felt about as muscular as wet bathroom tissue.

Somehow we managed two formal run-throughs of our routine before Jenifer had to rush off to a three P.M. rehearsal with a real ballet dancer. I experienced several nanoseconds of sheer joy and exhilaration when I was able to keep her en pointe: It was, in *Swan Lake* terms, like flying alongside the most graceful bird under the sun. In the end, I was relieved that neither of us broke a wing or a leg.

That evening, I watched Charles and Jenifer perform *Intermezzo* at the New York State Theater. For the first time, I could truly appreciate the artistry and athleticism demanded by their magnificent pliés, pirouettes, leaps, and lifts. I went backstage, and gave Jenifer a congratulatory hug. Then Charles and I slung our tote bags over our shoulders like a couple of accountants who'd just completed a routine audit, and went out for a couple of beers.

Act Six

HOLLYWOOD, HOT DOGS, FIRE-EATING, AND WHITE WATER

A Day in the Life of an Extra, Er, Background Artist

I drove directly from LAX to the Hollywood Walk of Fame on a sun-thirsty Thursday afternoon, desperately seeking some luck of the break-a-leg variety. I was on a fanciful pursuit of show business fame and fortune that had suddenly turned serious. Back at JFK, the airline claimed I had canceled my $280 e-ticket. I had to fork over $980 to fly to Los Angeles in time to make my gig as an extra on the ABC sitcom *George Lopez*.

I located George Lopez's star in front of a Banana Republic store. As I shuffled my feet across it, hoping his stardom might rub off, I attracted the notice of a sidewalk performer who said he was a magician and bard. He made a white handkerchief disappear into thin air, and then he quoted Shakespeare: "All that glisters is not gold, / Often have you heard that told; / Many a man his life hath sold."

The following morning at 8:30, I arrived at Stage Four on the Warner Brothers lot in Burbank. The otherwise unimposing tan stucco-walled building was one of Hollywood's most hallowed halls. In addition to being the place where *George Lopez* was taped, it was where scenes in *Casablanca, Mildred Pierce,* the original *Ocean's Eleven,* and *Murphy Brown* were shot.

Upon entering Stage Four, I was instructed to join a score of other *George Lopez* extras on the bleachers overlooking the sitcom's interior sets. The second assistant director, Paul Coderko, informed us that we would be playing the parts of workers in the fictional Powers Brothers aircraft factory. He quickly added that we were not mere extras but "background artists" whose contributions were essential to the show's success.

"In this business there's a food chain, and background artists like you are generally at the bottom," he said. "I've found that if I treat you with respect, you'll help me out when I need you to."

Paul explained that we were shooting the finale of the show's sixth season, a cliffhanger episode scheduled to air on ABC in May 2007. The Powers brothers had sold their factory to a Mexican tycoon who planned to import cheap foreign labor. We workers believed that George Lopez, the factory manager, would fight to keep our jobs. Instead, George was going to double-cross us by accepting a six-figure salary to relocate to another factory in Phoenix.

After reporting to wardrobe to pick up my work shirt, I quickly discovered that my modest role demanded more backgrounding and more artistry than I ever imagined. On six separate occasions, my fellow workers and I were to shout lines or cheer in unison. Most of the time, however, we had to pretend to be working and talking to one another without actually uttering any words. All this make-believe was aimed at creating a moving tableau to help sell the foreground action as "real."

In the first of our three scripted scenes, we were to hold newspapers, ostensibly searching for jobs to replace the ones we were about to lose. At the call for action, I was to walk across the factory floor, point out some promising want ads to a pair of female workers, and silently lip-synch a conversation. "Don't try to walk and read at the same time," Paul advised. "Glance at the paper, then look up and walk."

Ada Bey, a longtime background artist who doubled as a coordinator, added another degree of difficulty.

"Make sure you don't rustle those newspapers," she said. "We're on a sound stage, and any noise carries."

The script called for George to enter the factory and immediately order us to get back to work. The problem was, there was nothing real for us to do. All the "machinery" was either antiquated and inoperable or just plain fake. Here again, quiet was at a premium. "If it makes noise, don't touch it," Ada cautioned.

I found a three-inch set of wires that resembled a miniature abacus lying on a workbench. I picked it up and held it against the side of a defunct machine. A female worker strode up with a pad and pencil, and nudged my shoulder as if to collect some kind of measurement data.

In our second scene, we were to camp in the factory to protest its sale to the Mexican tycoon. At this point, George would pretend to be back on our side. He would enter the factory talking on a cell phone to a radio station that was publicizing our protest. He would then hold up the phone and ask us to name our favorite deejays.

"Dr. Funkenstein and Rodney!" we would shout.

But that was just a comic setup. George would cover the cell phone, and remind us that he had already spoken with Dr. Funkenstein and Rodney. He was now talking to another pair of deejays, Captain Stan and the Monkey Man.

"Captain Stan and the Monkey Man!" we would shout, correcting ourselves in the nick of time.

In our final scene, we were to curl up on sleeping bags spread across the factory floor and pretend to sleep. During rehearsal, one of my coworkers actually did fall asleep. I thought this might be the ultimate in method acting. But he later confided that he had been up all night working as a background artist on a Nicole Kidman movie.

That reminded me of my financial plight. A non-union background artist was paid about $60 a day. As it happened, I had earned a Screen Actors Guild card back in 1990 for a one-line performance in the film *Regarding Henry* that wound up on the cutting room floor. But even as a union member, I was due only $126 unless I managed to get another one-line speaking part. In that case, I'd make $713 for the day. (Under the rules, shouting in unison with fourteen other people does not constitute a speaking part.)

I got the break-a-leg luck I was looking for in hair and makeup. As the stylist coiffed what was left of my golden locks, George came in and gave me a hug. Like just about everyone else on the set, he had heard about my ticketing problem at JFK. He was also an avid golfer who had recently been host of the PGA Tour's Bob Hope Chrysler Classic, and he'd heard that I'd briefly played as a professional on the mini-tours.

"I'll take care of you, man," he promised. "Us golfers got to stick together."

That afternoon, the scriptwriters said they wanted to insert a transition line after my fellow factory workers and I shouted "Captain Stan and the Monkey Man!" I was told to ask George to "get us some T-shirts." A dialogue coach advised, "You can elaborate on the line a little bit if you want."

"How about, 'Hey, man, get us some T-shirts?'" I asked.

The dialogue coach nodded approvingly. It wasn't, "We'll always have Paris," but it would do.

The studio audience arrived for the live taping at five P.M. Along with George and the principal players, my fellow background artists and I were on the set until almost nine P.M. shooting and reshooting scenes. But I said my one line without a hitch. I was so intent on making some money to help pay for my exorbitant airfare that I simply forgot about being nervous.

The following morning, I stopped by the Hollywood Walk of Fame. The magician-bard I'd met two days before was nowhere in sight. Instead, I encountered an escape artist equipped with a straitjacket and handcuffs who said he had been working the sidewalks for over forty years. I filled him in on my star-crossed turn as a background artist and asked if I had any realistic hope of achieving fame and fortune in show business. "It takes energy, drive, and most of all desire," he allowed.

I shuffled my feet across George Lopez's star in a last ritual act of gratitude. Then I said farewell to the escape artist, and drove back to LAX filled with newfound energy and a desire to demand a refund from the airline.

Hawking Hot Dogs: Some Are All-Stars and Then There's . . .

I hopped off the No. 7 subway train at Shea Stadium trying to transform my native Texas twang into Queens-accented English. It was shortly before eleven A.M. on a Saturday in April, about 55 degrees, with a chilly northwest wind. The New York Mets were warming up to play the Washington Nationals at one P.M., and I was warming up to sell a food item as famously American as baseball and apple pie.

"Hawt dawgs," I muttered. "Getchur red-hawt hawt dogs."

I hustled over to the stadium employee entrance, where would-be vendors dressed in black pants, shoes, and shirts were forming three lines. The line on the left was for members of the Office and Professional Employees International Union. The middle line was for experienced nonunion workers. I joined the line on the right composed mainly of newcomers like me.

Almost everyone back at headquarters, including the Boss, had wondered how selling hot dogs qualified as an executive pursuit. To me, it seemed like a no-brainer for any executive who loves baseball. Hot dog vendors get to watch games free, interact with the fans, and make some money while they're at it. I figured it as an entertaining—and easy—divertissement.

I began to realize how wrong I was when I encountered Tom Morely, the blond-mustached Aramark vending manager. Vending was a "spec" job: Applicants showed up hoping there was work available and that their appearance met with Tom's approval. Tom noted that I was out of uniform in my snowboarding jacket, jeans, and blue sweater. But as I had agreed to donate my hot dog vending proceeds to charity, he gave me a pass. I naïvely asked what kind of training I would receive.

"T.B.F.," he replied, lighting a cigarette. "We're talking trial by fire."

As I slipped through the employee entrance, I tried to dispel thoughts of impending immolation by thinking dollars and sense. Despite the popularity of vegetarian foods, hot dogs made of precooked beef or pork trimmings were still big business. According to the National Hot Dog and Sausage Council, a meat industry trade group, American consumers spent more than $3.9 billion on hot dogs and sausages in supermarkets in 2006. But the most lucrative markets were baseball stadiums.

"Americans will eat enough hot dogs at major league ballparks this year to stretch from RFK Stadium in Washington, D.C., to AT&T Park in San Francisco," the council claimed.

Shea Stadium led all major league ballparks with annual consumption of more than 1.5 million hot dogs. (Yankee Stadium, interestingly enough, was not ranked among the top ten.) According to Aramark, most of Shea's dogs were sold by forty-eight vendors who roamed the stands, as opposed to concessionaires who sold from fixed locations. The average vendor sold 150 a game, and 10,000 to 12,000 a season. Working for commissions ranging from 13 percent to 16 percent, depending on seniority, they could make $150 to $200 a game, and as much as $30,000 a season.

I met a sampling of my fellow vendors as we wended through the bowels of the stadium. Along with several minimum-age eighteen-year-olds from the Bronx and Queens, they included a school principal, an accountant, a day trader, a bus driver, and Bobby Lee, a forty-eight-year-old retired New York City fireman who had relocated to Kansas City but still commuted to Shea to work baseball games. "I've been doing this since 1974 because I just love the Mets," Bobby explained.

At noon, I reported to the so-called money room on the stadium's field level. It featured a row of teller windows where I exchanged a $50 bill for a roll of quarters and a stack of $5 bills. Tom Morely provided me with a black apron, a black cap, a greenish-yellowish T-shirt with VENDOR on the back, and a plastic button marked "4.75," signifying the price of a hot dog, sans dollar sign.

I proceeded to a bustling commissary redolent with the aroma of freshly popped popcorn. In lieu of formal training, Tom paired me with Arnold Henriguez, twenty-seven, a recent York College graduate. Arnold was a ten-year veteran who had sold enough hot dogs the previous season to qualify as the Mets' designated vendor at the 2006 All-Star Game in Pittsburgh.

We hurried to the back of the commissary where a porter was loading each steel bin with a can of lighted Sterno, 30 hot dogs, 30 plastic packaged buns, 30 foil wraps, 30 paper napkins, packets of mustard and ketchup, and a long metal fork. Arnold patiently tutored me in the proper food-handling "barrier" technique. I was supposed to grab a foil wrap with one hand and grab the fork with the other, use the fork to split open a bun and place it in the wrap, and then spear a hot dog and place it inside the bun.

"The thing that's going to be challenging is separating the buns without touching them with your bare hands," Arnold said.

In fact, bun splitting proved to be only one of many unexpected challenges for me. Hot dog vendors must balance their bins on the tops of their caps when they parade through the stands. My fully loaded bin weighed forty pounds, but it felt heavier than Sisyphus's rock. With each step, I feared that I was going to trip and fall, igniting a Sterno-fueled trial by fire in which I perished amid sizzling meat, flaming dough, and melting plastic.

To my relief, most of the Mets fans in the field boxes to which I was assigned recognized that I was a rookie vendor, and took a kind of bemused pity on me. My first customer was Steve Plotnicki, a food industry blogger with a nameplate on his box. I mentioned that my day job was writing. "Fantastic," he replied. "This is like ordering a hot dog from Hemingway."

Moments later, a fellow sitting a few rows behind Mr. Plotnicki gave me my first tip, a crisp dollar bill. "I like the way you handle those buns," he said, grinning.

As I hoisted the bin back on top of my cap, I heard cries for hot dogs from customers on every side. I all but abandoned proper barrier technique in a frantic effort to supply the surging demand. I got my second tip, a whopping $5, from a stockbroker named Joel Klein. By the top of the third inning, I had only two hot dogs left. As this happened to be Kids Day at Shea, I gave them away to a pair of eleven-year-old boys.

I retreated to the commissary for a refill, only to find that Arnold was on his third bin, and Bobby Lee had sold 150 sticks of cotton candy. "Move it," Bobby hollered. "You're getting paid by the piece, not by the hour."

By the time I returned to the stands carrying a second bin, my arms and legs felt like rubber hot dogs, and my hastily affected Queens accent had become a mournful wheeze. Worse, the Mets were losing to the Nationals, and I hadn't managed to see a single pitch. Nine hot dogs later, I decided to turn in my bin and watch the game.

At the bottom of the seventh, I went to the money room for the inevitable accounting. Arnold the All-Star had sold 180 hot dogs, netting more than $136, not including tips. I had moved a measly 39 hot dogs, including sales and giveaways, losing a total of $29.75. "I can send you to a minor-league park in Brooklyn," Tom Morely said, exhaling a puff of cigarette smoke, "or I can just fire you."

I reckoned I deserved the latter, and we shook hands on it. Then I slunk away, back to the No. 7. As the train pulled into Grand Central, I reached into my jacket pocket and found a solitary fork-shredded bun.

"Hawt dawg," I muttered. "I need a red-hawt hawt dog."

Where the School Lunch Menu Includes Fire and Swords

I hobbled down the Coney Island boardwalk in the footsteps of all the sideshow freaks who had come and gone before. The sun glinted off the Cyclone roller coaster and the carousels. Flags flapped in the wind. Mothers pushed baby carriages. Couples strolled arm in arm past hot dog stands, piña colada huts, and potholes strewn with broken glass.

The crowd hardly noticed as I clutched my crutches and sidled down the 12th Street ramp. My only visible deformity was a heavily bandaged left foot that resembled a reptile claw, thanks to a protruding metal pin surgically inserted to repair my hammertoe. Nothing suggested that I was on an executive pursuit that would transform me into a fire-eating human blockhead.

I slipped through a steel door near the corner of Surf Avenue, and entered a 1917 vintage auditorium that houses the Coney Island Sideshow School. It featured some wooden bleachers occupied by a dozen fellow students, black walls covered with murals depicting sword swallowers and snake charmers, and a stage equipped with a faux electric chair.

Todd Robbins, forty-three, the dean of the school, bounded onto the stage. Six feet four inches tall, with blond hair, a black vest, and a mischievous grin, he was wielding a hundred-year-old Moroccan sword. "Most people think sword swallowing is fake, but it's the most dangerous act in the sideshow," he declared. "People have died trying to do this. I myself once ended up in the emergency room in Wichita, Kansas, at three A.M."

Todd tilted his head back, hoisted the sword over his mouth, and then lowered the tip. The blade was eighteen inches long and made of forged steel, but it seemed to slide down his throat as easily as a melting icicle. When the blade disappeared, he bowed forward from the waist to show the hilt protruding from his lips. Then he straightened up again and extracted the sword from his mouth. My fellow students and I applauded in wonder.

"All the acts you're going to learn this evening are

real," Todd assured us as he wiped the sword with a cloth. "They're based on principles of physics and anatomy. But since most people slept through physics and anatomy in high school, the secrets have been safe until now."

I felt my own throat tighten in nervous anticipation as Todd outlined the curriculum. Founded in 2002, the sideshow school offered courses in both spring and fall that consisted of five classes lasting from six P.M. to ten P.M. on weekdays. Subjects ranged from sword swallowing, in which you trained your throat to overcome its natural gag reflex, to lying on a bed of nails.

Todd's recounting of bizarre sideshow history was worth the $600 tuition. He noted that sideshows were a major form of entertainment on Coney Island and in much of America through the first half of the twentieth century. They were called ten-in-ones because they presented ten acts in one venue, typically a small tent or catwalk adjacent to the main carnival arena. Except for notorious frauds perpetrated by the likes of P. T. Barnum, many of the acts demanded actual feats of derring-do or people who were unabashed in displaying their so-called oddities.

Indeed, sideshows were among the nation's original countercultures, self-contained worlds with their own protocols and a three-rung hierarchy of performers.

The royalty were the highly paid "true freaks," people who were born with some kind of physical deformity. Two famous examples were Emmitt Bejano, the "Alligator Boy" with scaly skin caused by ichthyosis, and his wife "Percilla the Monkey Girl," who had abnormal hair growth. Married for fifty years, "Alligator Boy" and "Monkey Girl" ended up owning their own traveling sideshow.

The second rung of the hierarchy was occupied by "self-made freaks," people born looking pretty much like everyone else who did something to make themselves different. They ran the gamut from performers with full-body tattoos and piercings to those who created artificial deformities like elongated lips and necks.

The third rung consisted of "working acts," otherwise normal people who learned the dark secrets of acts like sword swallowing and fire-eating, many of which dated back thousands of years to the fakirs of India.

Todd himself was a working act. Born in Southern California, he had earned a theater degree and performed Shakespeare with the American Conservatory Theater in San Francisco. But at age twelve, he had become enamored of the magic of the sideshow. "I grew up in a safe, clean, unexciting suburb," he recalled. "I wanted to experience something extravagant, especially those acts that were real and did not involve some form of deception."

Realizing that the sideshow counterculture was dying out, Todd persuaded several old masters like Ward Hall to share their secrets. In 1991, he started performing at Coney Island. He had since become chairman of Coney Island USA, which operated a museum as well as the sideshow school. He had performed on television, at Carnegie Hall, and for major corporations like Fujifilm, Salomon Smith Barney, and General Electric. Among his stunts was eating GE lightbulbs, which he described as "very risky because you're playing Russian roulette with your intestinal tract for the next two days—if the broken glass doesn't pass through it can penetrate the lining and cause you to bleed to death."

I commenced my study of sideshow acts by becoming a "human blockhead," a stunt that called for me to jam a nail up my nose. Todd wisely started me off with a Q-tip, and a reassuring explanation of the secret involved. Contrary to popular misconception, he noted, the human nasal cavity goes straight back rather than straight up. He showed me how to locate the proper passage by keeping the Q-tip parallel to the floor. Sparing the gory details, suffice it to say that I made the Q-tip disappear, and later managed to cover half of a six-inch nail.

Presently, we turned to fire-eating, a decidedly more dangerous stunt. "Kids, don't try this at home—wait until you get to school," Todd joked. Then he added in a cautionary tone, "This is not for everyone. Occasionally, it throws people off, but if it does, we'll find a way to get you through it."

The tools required in fire-eating were a torch consisting of a metal stick with a wad of cotton fabric on the tip, a jar of camper stove fluid, and a match. The obvious hazards included singeing your lungs by inhaling the flame and blistering your lips on the torch. But by now I was willing to put my trust in Todd and his prescribed step-by-step approach.

First, I dipped the cotton end of the torch into the camper stove fluid, and shook off the excess. I tilted my head back, and licked my lips. Then I opened my mouth, took a deep breath, and held it. Todd lit my torch with a match. "Now put the torch in your mouth, close your lips, and keep them closed until I say okay," he instructed. "That will put the fire out by depriving it of oxygen."

Next thing I knew, I devoured the first torch, then a second and a third. The only slightly unpleasant aftereffects were a slight stinging in the back of my throat caused by the heat of the flames, and what my long-suffering wife later described as "horribly bad breath" caused by the camper stove fluid. I'd found my sideshow métier—and something else I hadn't expected.

"I've challenged you to expand your perceptions and how far you can stretch the boundaries of what is doable in your own life, " Todd said. "The desire to find out what is possible is what makes people go out and do great things."

A few minutes later, I hobbled back out onto the Coney Island boardwalk and hoisted my crutches in jubilation, a solitary fire-eating human blockhead waving his freak flags at the starry sky.

Tuck Forward, Chill Out, and
Wait for the Hands of God

My white-water kayaking instructor Jon Clark pointed at a ledge of jagged rocks called Nantahala Falls. It was a warm July afternoon in westernmost North Carolina, and we were perched on an overlook beside Highway 19 outside Bryson City. Outfitted in plastic helmets, wet suits, and synthetic rubber spray skirts, we looked like a couple of bionic mushrooms sprouting between stands of hemlock, sycamore, and beech trees.

The section of the Nantahala River below us appeared to be a boiling cauldron. Gray mists curled up from frothing currents punctuated by bubbling hydraulic holes. But I knew it was just an illusion. The water was flowing from the bottom of a dam about nine miles upstream at 650 cubic feet per second, and its temperature was a chilling 54 degrees Fahrenheit.

"I think you can make it if you stay close to that triangle rock on the right," Jon allowed.

I squinted at the triangle rock, shivering. Over the preceding twenty-four hours, Jon and his colleagues at the Nantahala Outdoor Center had given me a crash course in the basics of white-water kayaking. I'd practiced on a flatwater section of the Chattooga River, where the movie *Deliverance* was shot, and I'd run some Class II rapids on the Nantahala River. But Nantahala Falls was a full-fledged Class III rapids, and I was still a rank novice.

My head reeled from the conflicting advice of two inner voices. One part of me feared that a premature attempt to run the falls might result in serious injury or even death. Another part of me insisted that the opportunity to take a calculated risk was what made this—and life in general—worthwhile executive pursuits. The voice of that second part came out of my mouth.

"Let's do it," I said.

Jon grinned and patted the top of my helmet. Then we marched back to the concrete beach upstream where we had temporarily parked our kayaks. Even as my more cautious inner voice screamed for me to reconsider, I recalled the signature line of the thrill-seeking Atlanta suburbanite played by Burt Reynolds in *Deliverance:* "Sometimes you have to lose yourself before you find anything."

For all my trepidation, I realized that I'd already found something extraordinary in the sport of kayaking. I was not alone. According to the Outdoor Industry Foundation, a nonprofit trade group based in Boulder, Colorado, over 15 million Americans annually participated in paddle sports, which include canoeing and various forms of kayaking. The foundation reported that over 2.2 million people, roughly 40 percent of them under age twenty-four, participated in white-water kayaking.

In contrast to more popular but much tamer recreational flatwater kayaking, white-water kayaking offered a high-risk adrenaline rush as well as almost unlimited opportunities for adventure. At age twenty-five, Jon Clark had been kayaking for over a decade in well-traveled and uncharted waters in North and South America. "For me, it's all about enjoying a beautiful experience on a river that you can't get to any other way," he told me. "There's nothing like spending seven or eight days on a river where you don't know what's around the next bend."

The Nantahala Outdoor Center was widely acclaimed as the nation's premier paddling school.

Nestled at the intersection of the eponymous river and the Appalachian Trail, the center had an outfitting store, lodging, three restaurants, and access to seven local waterways. The instructional staff included several former Olympians and world-class trick kayakers known as play boaters. A two-day beginners' course cost $456, equipment rental, meals, and lodging included. A single-day "white-water sampler" course that included lunch but no lodging was just $99.

Before we ventured onto a river, Jon acquainted me with the five pieces of equipment essential to kayaking, the first of which is the boat itself, a fiberglass shell measuring about eight feet in length. The second key piece of equipment is the spray skirt, which fits over your torso and is attached to the cockpit so as to keep water out of the kayak and you in it. Completing the ensemble are a double-bladed paddle, a helmet, and a padded life jacket known as a personal flotation device.

During our first session on water, Jon prepared me for the otherwise frightening experience of "going over," a kayaking term for involuntarily flipping your boat upside down. He deliberately flipped over my kayak, and had me hold my breath underwater for up to fifteen seconds. I was supposed to tuck forward to reduce the chances of banging my helmet against a rock. Then I was supposed to "chill out" to forestall a panic attack, and simply wait for him to come to my rescue.

"We call these 'the hands of God,' " Jon said when he flipped my kayak right side up again.

After the initial submergence exercises, Jon guided me through a self-righting technique called an "Eskimo roll" that required a vigorous hip twist and a deftly coordinated paddle stroke. He also tutored me in a much easier emergency maneuver called a "wet escape." All I had to do was pull the release strap of my spray skirt and swim away from the kayak. But he cautioned me not to ground my feet or I might get entrapped between piles of rocks and drowned by onrushing currents.

I all but forgot about the omnipresent dangers of kayaking at the outset of our second session on the Nantahala River. We put in amid a V-shaped gorge canopied with green leaves. Jon coached me to paddle using the big muscles of my torso instead of relying solely on my hands and arms. We cruised without upset through alternating sections of flatwater and Class II rapids more or less equivalent to foot-high ocean breakers.

"A little float and then a little foam!" I cried out with glee.

"Oh, yeah!" Jon exclaimed.

But both of us turned stone-cold serious when it came time to attempt Nantahala Falls. As we re-boarded our kayaks on the concrete beach upstream from the overlook, Jon reiterated his belief that I had a good chance of making it. But he nevertheless advised me to stick on some rubber nose clips, and asked me to review my submergence procedure.

"Tuck, chill, and wait for the hands of God," I said.

Jon nodded, and led the way down a relatively smooth channel that funneled into the falls from the right side of the river.

What happened next will forever remain a bitter-sweet blur in my memory. I saw Jon smoothly negotiate the falls about twenty yards ahead of me. Then I saw the treacherous triangle rock rising out of the foam. As per Jon's instructions, I knew I was supposed to lean into the rock to keep my kayak stable. But that move proved too counterintuitive for my novice abilities. I saw the bow of the boat careening out of control to the left. Then I felt a sharp slap against my nose and cheeks as I flipped over.

I spent the ensuing nine seconds tumbling over the falls upside down and backward. Although I failed to tuck, I somehow managed to remain calm for about six seconds. Instead of seeing my life flash before my eyes, all I saw was murky gray water and some brown blobs that resembled the overstuffed pillows on the couch in my home office.

The last three seconds of my submersion were flooded with rapidly increasing despair. Then I felt a tug on my kayak from somewhere above.

Suddenly, I found myself sitting upright in the cockpit, my face and body reverberating with aftershocks. As promised, Jon had come to my rescue with "the hands of God." I saw a crowd of people sitting on the riverbank just beyond the falls. They were cheering and applauding.

"Oh, yeah!" Jon exclaimed, patting the top of my helmet.

I spit out a mouthful of water and replied in kind.

"Oh, yeah!" I hollered. "I've been delivered!"

ACKNOWLEDGMENTS

I am grateful to all those who inspired, supported, and participated in the journalism that led to this book, especially: Charles Askegaard, Jacob and Angela Arabo, Victor Ayad, Patricia Birch, Olga Berluti, Ada Bey, Michael Blick, Boris the Barber, Brandy Library, Chris Briere, Bruce Cameron Clark, Ron Colangelo, Steve Cone, Paul Corderko, Lienette Crawfoord, John Damgard, Chris Delgatto, Dockside Bar & Grill, Linda Dozoretz, Richie Frisella Sr., Alexander Gabriel, Emma Gilby, Rob Gregory, Marc Grossberg, Jimmy Gubelman, George Gurley, Arnold Henriguez, Frank Hentic, Ives and Pandy Hentic, Matt Higgins, Michael Humphrey, Alison Becker Hurt, Harrison Hurt, Lawrence Ingrassia, Joan Jett, Woody Johnson,

Alan Katzman, Bill Keller, Mitchell Kelly, Pete Kendall, Michael and Eleanora Kennedy, David and Julia Koch, Brenda Lambert, Lee Lauderback, Sean Laverty, Bobby Lee, John Loeffler, George Lopez, Lumi Restaurant, Eric Mangini, Justin McCareins, Victoria McKee, Phyliss Messinger, Jason Michael, David Moldawer, Tom Morely, Belita Moreno, Nantahala Outdoor Center, the New York City Ballet, the New York Jets, the New York Mets, P. J. O'Rourke, Patrick Ottomani, Chad Pennington, Bart Richardson, Jenifer Ringer, Todd Robbins, Stanley Rumbough, Amy Sacco, James Salter, Arthur O. Sulzberger Jr., Gay Talese, Sandra Van Meek, Alex Ward, Thayer Whipple, Tim Yan, Dr. Nelson Ying, and most of all James Impoco, Erik Olsen, Theodore B. Conklin III, Meine Muse, and Mickey Meece, the best editor and dearest friend a writer could ever have.